THE COUNTRY GARDEN

THE
COUNTRY
GARDEN
JOHN BROOKES

PHOTOGRAPHS BY
JACQUI HURST

DORLING KINDERSLEY LONDON

Senior editor David Lamb
Art editor Meryl Lloyd

Editor Heather Dewhurst

Editorial director Jackie Douglas
Art director Roger Bristow

First published in Great Britain in 1987
by Dorling Kindersley Publishers Limited,
9, Henrietta Street, London WC2E 8PS

British Library Cataloguing in Publishing Data

Brookes, John
   The country garden.
   1. Gardens   2. Gardening
   I. Title
   635   SB454

ISBN 0-86318-255-0

Typeset by Modern Text Typesetting

Reproduced by Colorscan, Singapore

Printed in Italy by A. Mondadori, Verona

CONTENTS

THE NEW COUNTRY GARDEN

It is undoubtedly true that there is an increasing number of
people who seek to live in the country. This desire has been created by all
sorts of social situations and conditioning, none more than the
decay within many of our inner cities, and the numbing sameness of our
vast suburban sprawl. Many are now freed from their city desks by
new technologies and can look to the country for a fresh life-style.
But when they do move, what is to stop what was the
countryside becoming further surburban sprawl, if not in terms of new
building, in the way gardens are gardened? It is high time for a
new look at the country garden.

Causes for concern

Many will, in fact, be disappointed with the countryside
they move to, holding a romantic image of it in their mind's eye,
painted from summer jaunts. The hard fact is that much of the countryside
is impoverished. High-output chemical agriculture has led to hedgeless
landscapes, inert soils and fewer and fewer farm workers, leaving
many villages bereft of young blood. The new country-dweller has to be
informed. Country living is more than logs and lambs, it is a way of
life conditioned by the all-pervading surroundings, and in most
countries those surroundings change very quickly from area to area,
depending on the geology and traditional methods of farming. Country-
livers must be prepared to become part of the scene and strengthen
it, or our countryside will be lost.

The new country look

Plants that no time ago were considered weeds, now have a place in
casual-looking mixed plantings. You would include them in a country flower
arrangement, why not in a country garden?

Thankfully, there is now a growing concern for the welfare of the countryside, including a concern for the conservation and preservation of native flora and fauna whose habitats are under constant threat.

Most new building in the countryside is the result of the same rationalization of farm land that leads more and more to unmanageable lots being parcelled off to home owners. Subsequently, new country gardeners often have a plot of illogical dimensions.

They manage their land themselves, between work and a whole range of other recreational activities, and expect to holiday abroad perhaps, leaving the garden once if not twice a year, and so want as many machines as possible to aid them.

Country style gardening

The new country garden is a response to all of these trends. It provides an easy-to-maintain look—a new, essentially country style that can appear random, even unkempt, because beneath the romantic appeal there lies a practical framework.

It is far from being just a summer flower garden. It is one which draws its inspiration from its own location, be it agricultural landscape, rugged moorland, woodland, or any of the many permutations of landscape types. It is a form of gardening that takes a closer look at what grows wild and how it grows, at traditional walls, fences and hedge types, then uses and reflects it to produce a garden that is a visual bonus to its locality.

It is very much the other end of the spectrum to the garden-centre, supermarket approach to gardening, which would have our gardens conforming to a universal suburban standard, summed up by all the tackiness that terms such as "patio living" engender. Why should the millions who live and garden in the country (not in stately homes, but in ordinary cottages and houses), and those who want to include country style in their town garden, conform to such a standard with its carrot fly and conifer obsession?

The apartment dweller's dream
Many apartment dwellers have had an alternative country residence for some time. This is a Finnish summer home that provides the perfect magical antidote to city living.

GARDENS IN A LANDSCAPE

The country garden is part of its surroundings in a way its smaller urban counterpart can never be. The country house and its land are not only part of the social community, but they also contribute significantly to the look of the countryside.

Creating and maintaining a country garden encompasses much more than just horticulture and recreation, it is a matter of husbandry—a nice-sounding word, embodying concern. If you have an older property, such concern is for what you have inherited—features such as old trees, ancient walls, and streams or ditches that you care for within your boundaries, but which are part of a much larger network. And concern not only for the structure and plants of your garden, but also for the wide variety of wildlife it attracts.

There is in the country much more of an awareness of before and after, a strong sense of how very transitory we are, scratching away at the few surface inches that we husband during our spell. Instant town gardens can be great fun, but country gardens deserve a long commitment so they can mature like good wine.

TRADITIONAL HUSBANDRY
There will be a traditional form of husbandry, tried and tested by time, ideally suited to the location of your country garden. It will be tempered by your soil and its underlying rock, along with the weather and altitude. To deny traditional husbandry is costly, foolhardy and will keep you ignorant of the spirit of your garden's place, its *genius loci*—the feel of the surrounding landscape that you must come to understand fully if you are to make a really successful country garden.

Your garden as part of the landscape *The scale, planting and "feel" of a surrounding landscape must influence the mood of the garden. How futile to try to improve on the ambience of a location such as the English valley shown left, or to make a decorative show of flowers around the bean and pea-sticks in the garden, right.*

HISTORICAL REVIEW

There have been various schools of thought on the place of a garden within its landscape and their subsequent inter-relationship. The earliest gardens were retreats from the "awe"fulness of nature, for it was overwhelming to a tiny rural commmunity. Its wildness was excluded by high walls or hedges, and within the enclosure our forefathers created their ordered, formal layouts, clipped and neat, as a statement of their superiority and control over nature's seeming disorder. Geometric patterns alone seemed to amuse, with little horticultural content.

Seventeenth-century enclosed garden *The small, enclosed garden of the seventeenth century consisted of box-edged beds containing a limited palette of decorative garden plants arranged in a geometric pattern. Such a formal garden would have been based on similar designs developed in Holland, France and Italy and set out to man's control over nature.*

This formal tradition extended its limits, and there were permutations of the idea of the enclosed garden through-out sixteenth- and seventeenth-century Europe. The most extensive garden patterns eventually escaped their enclosing walls, and the lines of the geometric layouts were extended into surrounding forest, by out-rides on the Continent and by planted avenues of trees in England where, by the seventeenth century, indigenous forest had been severely denuded for the building of ships and houses. To be successful visually, however, extensive avenues require flat ground, and from the etchings available of the larger formal layouts in England, the young plantings looked bizarre progressing uphill and down dale.

IDEALIZED LANDSCAPE GARDENS
Towards the end of the seventeenth century in England, with the influences of Italian landscape painting and highly

romanticized ideas about the life of the noble peasant, there began to be an appreciation of natural landscape. The interest was fuelled by literature and a concern for Palladian architecture, which, fashion dictated, should be surrounded by parkland in the new "improved" landscape style. The pastoral landscape was allowed to flow to the very walls of the houses so that the views from the mansion, sitting proud and four-square within its domain, were into a controlled landscape, furnished with incidents of Classical origin. Streams were damned to become lakes that reflected this idealized pastoral image and views were moulded by mass planting of indigenous trees. The idea of using decorative, exotic plants, and of the decorative garden, was still to be realized but towards the end of the eighteenth century, foreign plant material began to find its way back from the furthest edges of the British empire.

COTTAGE GARDEN TRADITION
There was still a very strict social order pertaining to country life, with the great landlord or squire being the employer, and the remainder of society in his employ, except for the vicar, doctor and school teacher, who stood somewhere on the sidelines. The "big house" garden dominated, and if it was grand enough might have survived to be included on today's round of stately garden tours. But this is not to say that there were no more humble gardens. There was a continuing smaller or cottage garden tradition, which had probably not changed very much since medieval times, in which plants (many of them herbal), were grown for decorative, culinary and medicinal purposes, along with vegetables that were grown solely for domestic use. The planning was haphazard and there was certainly no room for lawns.

The landscape garden *The rolling 'improved' landscape of the eighteenth-century parkland garden, was the antithesis of the introspective, protected seventeenth-century garden. Armies of manual labourers were required to subtly remould slopes, shape lakes, plant out groups of indigenous trees and punctuate the whole with decorative Classical incidents, such as temples and statuary.*

The nineteenth century saw enormous social changes and with it the emergence of a new middle class, whose villa homes and smaller gardens created the earliest suburbs. Emphasis was placed on education, particularly concerning things scientific, including botany. Plant exploration became *de rigueur* and the botanic garden was required to show off the latest finds. A whole new horticultural spectrum was on offer, and the nineteenth-century plantsman turned his back on the countryside, put up the barriers again and within them grew the newly-introduced exotic species — plants which in their maturity were bound to make the Victorian garden appear alien to its surroundings. Brilliant colour was introduced in geometrically planned beds of annuals and conifers. Rhododendrons and camellias were imported and planted at random (often within the landscape park of the previous century) to create a look that is now considered altogether native in many parts of England.

The Victorian garden *The typical Victorian look was in a style known as "gardenesque". Exotic trees such as the monkey puzzle (Araucaria araucana) were mixed with spectacularly colourful and intricate arrangements of carpet bedding. The conservatory was the home of a further collection of exotics that were too tender for the winter frosts of the outdoor climate.*

TWENTIETH-CENTURY REACTION
At the beginning of the twentieth century there was a reaction to the blatant artificialy of the nineteenth-century look. In Victorian England millions had moved

from the country to the town and as a result, rural life and the countryside were idealized in intellectual circles, giving rise to the Arts and Crafts movement, which pioneered a return to traditional skills and materials. The early twentieth-century garden, therefore, whilst including features of Classical, formal layout, was styled with a feeling for nature, using shrub and perennial plant material that was more suited to its surroundings and more suited to the smaller garden. The feel of the garden, however, was rustic but medieval—it was enclosed, with a layout that had very little to do with the surrounding countryside. Among this last group of gardens are Sissinghurst, in Kent, and Hidcote Manor in Gloucestershire—English models for the country garden worldwide, but made at a time when labour and land were cheap.

Along with a genuine concern for the environment, the economics of the second part of the twentieth century has conditioned the country gardener to reconsider his smaller plot more as part of the landscape in which it sits. The new country garden is allowed to flow through its boundaries, is managed with an eye on tradition but using machinery as an aid, and, furthermore, it fulfills the practical requirements imposed by its users.

The early twentieth-century garden *By the turn of the twentieth century, country garden styling became more rural in fact, although still medieval in its fondness for the garden as a closed room. Planting was full and flowery, and there was a strong sense of tradition through the hard materials used for walls, paving, gates and doors, which were all finished to an exacting level of craftsmanship.*

UNDERSTANDING THE LANDSCAPE

The look of any landscape depends on its underlying geology: substrata of gravel, clay or rock, condition both the texture and the mineral content of the surface topsoil and hence its alkalinity or acidity. The nature of the topsoil in turn supports a natural vegetation that has allowed a certain type of agriculture or forestry to develop. In its turn, traditional local building, to house the people working on the land, was made using available materials — stone or brick, flint or wood — so that regional differences were very apparent.

Conservation is not only concerned with the preservation of the native flora and fauna of a pastoral region, it is also the preservation of its unique character. And it is into this regional tapestry that we insert the country garden.

As gardeners we should be interested in the way these same materials were used for walling and fencing. The local pavings are also relevant, and although one might not copy local style blindly, one might re-interpret it to suit particular requirements.

Similarly, in the selection of plant material, I am not proposing totally "wild" gardening to the exclusion of all else, but on the boundaries of your garden at least you will see how a knowledge of "wild" management is useful, and how native plant material is much easier to cultivate.

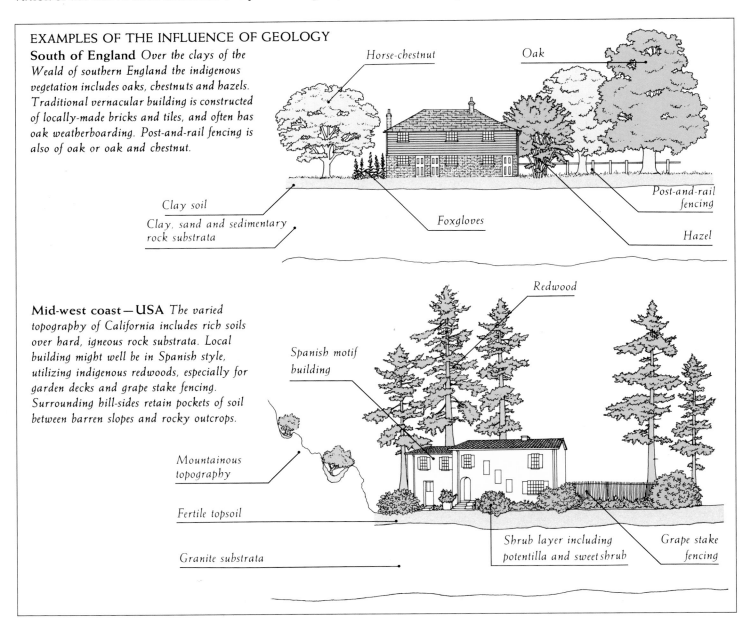

EXAMPLES OF THE INFLUENCE OF GEOLOGY

South of England *Over the clays of the Weald of southern England the indigenous vegetation includes oaks, chestnuts and hazels. Traditional vernacular building is constructed of locally-made bricks and tiles, and often has oak weatherboarding. Post-and-rail fencing is also of oak or oak and chestnut.*

Horse-chestnut

Oak

Clay soil

Clay, sand and sedimentary rock substrata

Foxgloves

Post-and-rail fencing

Hazel

Mid-west coast — USA *The varied topography of California includes rich soils over hard, igneous rock substrata. Local building might well be in Spanish style, utilizing indigenous redwoods, especially for garden decks and grape stake fencing. Surrounding hill-sides retain pockets of soil between barren slopes and rocky outcrops.*

Redwood

Spanish motif building

Mountainous topography

Fertile topsoil

Granite substrata

Shrub layer including potentilla and sweetshrub

Grape stake fencing

BORROWED LANDSCAPE

That your garden can be so much a part of its surroundings is surely a great advantage. Not only will any borrowed scenery beyond your boundary enlarge the apparent size of your plot, it should also serve as inspiration for your garden style, and help in the choice of materials both hard and soft.

The qualities and presence of some landscapes are so strong that they cannot be denied in gardens located within them. The character of such a landscape might be to do with its ground conformation or the extreme quality of a specific soil, which produces a particular vegetation; the presence of woodland, or the immense visual strength of a local material like stone or slate. Any of these strong natural characteristics has to be "used" within the concept of the garden, as imported, substitute forms will seem trivial and out of place.

But not all rural settings have an imposing strength, indeed most have quieter charms that can be just as worthwhile as the dominating landscape, and should similarly be used within your boundaries.

The quiet charms of an agricultural landscape *The gentle slopes of the Downs roll into this Sussex garden in southern England, with their swelling forms repeated in the foreground brick steps.*

VIEWS OUT

Since it is the natural landscape itself that entices most people to the countryside and encourages them to make their homes there, making the most of any view your country garden may have should be one of your first considerations when creating a new layout, or giving a face-lift to an older one.

But there is more to the job than simply removing a solid barrier for there are two further facts to consider. One is the prevailing weather direction (often the reason that the barrier was erected in the first place), and the other is the scale of the view compared with the scale of your garden. A small, "tamed" plot of land (your garden) set side-by-side with impressive-looking countryside, without a controlled transition between the two can result in the garden looking very insignificant indeed.

A panoramic view can be too much for the eye to encompass, and too expansive for day-to-day appreciation. There are ways to manipulate a view, whilst achieving the right balance between in and out, and at the same time providing weather protection. Seeing just a portion of a fine view, framed by vegetation, makes the transition from a wild landscape to a tamed one more digestible.

CONSIDERING A FRAME

Any framing of a view with vegetation or structure need not necessarily be on or close to the boundary of your garden, where it will emphasize its limits. Framing with planting nearer the viewpoint gives you greater control of the way you see the view, as illustrated in the diagrams opposite. It will also help you to avoid the common fault of evolving a garden design pattern that relates to the boundary, which only reinforces the feeling of enclosure. This means, for example, that if your boundary happens to be L-shaped, it is a mistake to base your garden layout on a series of concentric L-shapes that converge on your house, adjoining it at awkward angles. It is much better to relate your pattern and planting to the house—since it is from this point that you use the garden most, not only physically, but visually as well.

BALANCING SCALE

Controlling a view is also the way to regulate the change from the scale of the garden to the scale of the landscape beyond. There is a balance to be achieved. Framing and reducing the view will prevent what we make of the garden from appearing too trivial when seen against the broad sweep of either a natural or an agricultural landscape.

It will help to remember to keep any formal elements, symmetrical or asymmetrical (walling, paving, hedging and the like), in close proximity to the house or outbuildings, and repeating their lines. There is certainly no place for formal elements near the boundary, if you are trying to open up to a view, since the garden lines, shaping and planting should be as sympathetic to the landscape as possible, to strengthen the transition from in to out.

The space between the area close to the house and the boundary area is best treated in a loose manner, and the styling of its planting planned to progress from the more sophisticated or exotic near the structure (where it will be more sheltered), towards a wilder look the closer it gets to the landscape beyond (see also page 28).

Two-stage view (right) *In this Devonshire garden, planting frames the grazing immediately beyond the garden boundary, as well as a magnificent moorland view beyond that.*

Visual link (below) *The harmonious charm of this garden boundary depends on linear forms of lush garden planting echoing the horizontal lines of hedging and field shapes in the countryside.*

SHAPING A VIEW

To open up a panorama totally is, in most cases, too demanding visually and makes the site too exposed physically. Planting and structures in the garden can be used to shape the view, while at the same time giving protection. Secondary areas of interest can be created within the planting formations, near the viewpoint.

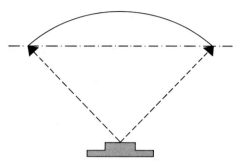

Exposed with a panoramic view

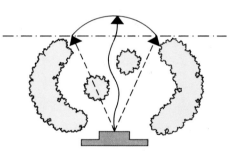

View held and masked

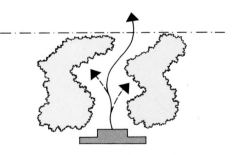

Serpentine planting to restrict the view

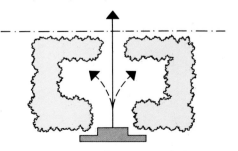

View formalized with symmetrical planting

INTEGRATING A VIEW

To integrate a view into a garden layout your general aim is to camouflage the actual boundary line, and to allow the feel of the countryside to run into your property.

Just making a hole in an existing hedge is not always the solution, for what remains of the hedge is still obviously the boundary. You need to plan planting inside the perimeter to bring the view through the hole that has been created, and to strengthen the visual link by counterbalancing any feature outside, with a feature inside.

You will have seen on page 19 how, if there is no existing solid barrier to mark a boundary, an effective way to integrate the view is to plan hedging, or the like, closer to

Making the garden visually stronger
Adding a second tree to the existing willow-leaf pear has the effect of strengthening the garden side of the garden/landscape equation. The view out is now divided by the tree grouping, and foreground garden planting is much reduced compared with the original.

Frame on the garden boundary *Clipped hedges, planted on the garden perimeter, have been shaped to have the effect of framing and holding the view. The position and shape of the hedging gives visual weight to the pear tree, making it an effective counterpoint to the restricted vista beyond.*

the viewpoint. You can then go on to align the piece of your own garden beyond it with the outside world, possibly treating it in a "natural" way with orchard, rough grass and wild flowers.

There are many permutations of this technique—but it is important to be clear in your own mind of the ultimate intention. Then it is important to plan or shape that intention, and finally to style it—that is, to give it the look and feel you think appropriate to your site (see also p.26).

Take another look at the larger photograph on pages 18 and 19, and then at the illustrations below. Each illustration shows an option for a different boundary treatment based on the inviting view shown in the photograph. Each version has a different intention, plan and styling. Those uninitiated in any form of garden design tend to turn the order of basic priorities round the wrong way, thinking first of styling, then plan, which with luck they hope will combine to produce an intention.

Bringing the landscape into the garden *The horizontal flow of the landscape, defined by its hedges, comes sweeping into the garden in this treatment that includes the planting of a foreground willow-leaf pear tree to counterbalance the existing one. Solid lawn planting on either side holds the view.*

The pear tree as a sculptural feature
With the clipped hedge frame close to the viewpoint, the pear tree becomes more of a sculptural feature sitting in the agricultural landscape. The trunk-encircling seat emphasizes the effect by strengthening the visual weight of the tree.

AXES AND VISTAS

Between the enclosed garden of the sixteenth and seventeenth centuries, and the eighteenth century landscape park, there was a transitional period of larger formal layouts, based on dominating axial pathways cut straight across the layout. These axes were often terminated by a dramatic vista of the countryside beyond.

In the nineteenth century, as ranges of alien plant material became available from foreign sources, it was fashionable to create a series of outside garden rooms enclosed by hedges, in which specific plant ranges could be grown. The planning of these outside rooms was again formal and often axial, with controlled vistas created by high planting. This is the tradition followed in the old country gardens at Hidcote manor in Gloucestershire and Sissinghurst Castle in Kent.

The formal axial tradition can create spectacular linear vistas out of the site—much of their attraction is the contrast between the clipped garden look and the free form of the wild or agricultural landscape beyond. While the vista can be grand and formal, the linear concept can also be re-interpreted more humbly in the manner of a straight path leading to a gate. The way it is paved, and then planted, styles the concept.

Pleached nut arch (right) *Although the styling of this inviting pathway is informal and rustic, the transition from garden to field is formal and axial. The contrast makes a very happy association.*

Informal grandeur (below) *There is an ancient, random quality to this formal build-up of levels to a gateway through the garden wall. The axial planning is reinforced by balanced planting on either side.*

GLIMPSED VIEWS

If your country garden is not blessed with notable panoramas (and this is the case for most of us), if a barn blocks your view from the house to farmland beyond, or if a public right of way ruins your best outlook, all is far from lost. There are invariably ways of using just a glimpse of the countryside to add significantly to the appeal of a part of your garden.

Such a glimpse might be through a distant gateway, between the trunks of trees or over the tops of shrubby plantings. They are delightful bonuses to encounter while strolling. To this end, the route of the path leading to the glimpse is important and might introduce an element of

surprise if the approach ensures that the glimpse is revealed at the last possible moment. Those using the path might be encouraged to slow down where they will notice the view out by the judicious siting of an inviting seat, or the landing to a generous flight of steps.

A gap between walls (right) *A planting of daisies (*Chrysanthemum maximum*) here masks a simple stile in a fenced gap between flint walls. The gap affords a tempting peek at light woodland beyond.*

A glimpse through planting (below) *A limited view of the countryside beyond foreground planting can be a bonus. This garden's boundary is beneath the far oak, but rough grass brings in the country feel.*

COUNTRY STYLING

So far we have considered the idea of a garden in the country being part of its location, how it should have some identity with its surroundings and fitness for place. But the country garden has also to serve its users and must be designed to that end, with pavings and terraces, with steps and storage spaces—all the necessities of the household, but outside. And it has to be practical in terms of both winter and summer use.

The uses to which you put different areas of the garden should reflect the progression from formal near the house, to wild at the boundary, as discussed on pages 18 and 19. The plan will become looser as it reaches the boundary where the garden fuses into its location. Each zone of the garden (see the diagram on p.28) will have defined uses, with the intermediate area (zone B) being largely reserved for recreation and/or decorative planting.

THE ULTIMATE LOOK
It is the way in which the plan for a garden is realized on site in bricks and mortar (or whatever) and then planted, that extends and brings to final fruition the style of the whole layout, creating a composition totally in sympathy with its ambience, both historically and geographically. Styling is all important for the ultimate look of a garden, but it starts with sound thinking about the layout.

STYLING CLOSE TO YOUR HOUSE
The style of the garden plan should not only reflect the location of the garden, but also the period of your house, particularly close to it in zone A (see p.28). Abstracted linear shapes, for example, are not generally

Faded grandeur (right) *The mood of the planting style of this garden is totally relaxed, although the selection of paving, seat and decorative features is grand to suit the backdrop of an ancient brick wall.*

Styling for today's garden (left) *An avenue of trees leading to an urn is a classic garden feature, but this inviting example has a scale and relaxed styling to suit the modern garden.*

considered appropriate for the garden surrounding a period building, though they would be suitable for a modern twentieth-century building. Free or natural shapes are correct for the linear patterns of an eighteenth-century park. More formal classic patterns befit a sixteenth- or seventeenth-century layout, and various permutations of these suit the nineteenth.

But is not only the line of a particular plan (the shape of the paths, terraces, lawns *et al*) that befits a garden to its period, it is also the scale and form of the areas the lines define. Provided that these are correct for a period, I believe there is room for a good deal of re-interpretation of period styles to suit twentieth-century living.

SUITABLE CONSTRUCTION DETAILS

We have seen how all the materials of house structure, its walls and fences, and the plants that surrounded it, were once indigenous—their massed effect is a chief ingredient in, for example, the strong characters of a mellow-stoned Gloucestershire hamlet or a limestone dales village. In the latter part of the twentieth century, however, we have a far greater range of materials from which to select, and far easier access to the builder's merchants and garden centres that supply them. It is a strange contradiction that those local materials we would ideally use are now often too expensive, so that we have to re-think what is suitable within the traditional context.

You will have to study styles of walling and coping, looking closely at the elevations of buildings to discern not only the types of material used but the way in which they were used and the styling of their details.

Even if you have to use new materials, make sure their use complies with traditional methods. This will help to unite your house with the garden near to it.

STYLING AND YOUR BOUNDARY

For the correct styling of your boundary area (zone C on p.28) you will need to turn your back to the house. At one time, the boundary area of a country garden would have been styled with the house and from the same palette of materials and plants. Now you can look to the shape and configuration of fields beyond, and note the prevalent

Planting close to the house *A conscious profusion of plants creates a softening random effect against architectural features. "Goldheart" ivy, climbing hydrangea and golden hop clothe the walls.*

THE ANATOMY OF A COUNTRY GARDEN

The process of styling your country garden will be considerably assisted by mentally dividing the plot into the three zones shown in this diagram. The approach is intended as a guide, not a set of rules, since in any particular garden unique qualities will require special treatment. In a small garden, for example, you could use the zone C treatment throughout.

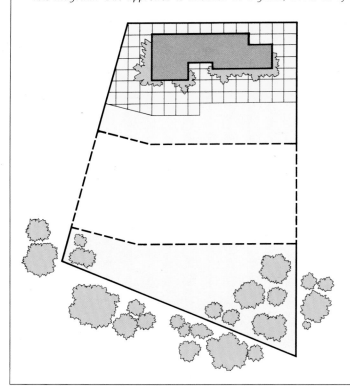

Zone A Area adjacent to building
This is the area reserved for any formal treatment that you may wish to give to your garden. The plan should be conceived to follow the form of the house, and realized in materials sympathetic to the structure. Planting can be bold in form and colour, but always in tune with the building.

Zone B Transitional area
In this zone, your style progresses from domestic to landscape in a way that suits the topography, weather and scale of the garden. This is the area that varies in size from garden to garden, depending on the overall size of the garden in question. It is often an area used for recreation with planting to suit, but tempered by the desired progression towards wilder planting as it approaches zone C.

Zone C Boundary area
The aim, in the boundary area, is to develop planting that is in complete sympathy with the countryside beyond so that the boundary line itself goes unnoticed. If you need a physical boundary, then it should be of a sort to match local types so that the effect is unobtrusive.

kinds of boundary, looking for clues. Study local plant formations, including hedge types, note the dominant species of solitary fieldtree, as well as those in surrounding woods and copses.

Most of us are probably aware of certain classic plant groups—heathers, heaths, birch and Scots pine on an acid soil, for example. There is, in northern Europe at least, a chalky soil association including wild clematis, native box, yew and euonymus (wayfaring tree), and on the Chilterns, in central southern England, one of beech with wild white cherry on the perimeter. On heavy clay soils hedging will be of thorn quicks, and ash and oak are the dominant trees.

Lowering your sights, look for wild plant types, gradually building a picture of the natural plant forms surrounding your garden. A good plant dictionary will point you to associated cultivated forms of the wild plants you have noted.

PLANTING AND STYLING

It is interesting that the different types of country garden planting often appear to be the strongest feature of country style. Everyone thinks of cottage style planting, for example, as the epitome of English country style. In fact, without the underlying structure of the style, the subsequent planting would probably not read nearly so strongly. It is very easy to be tempted to buy plants first, swayed by their immediate appeal, without being sure of the framework in which they will fit.

This is not to say that country gardening is not about plants. As you will see later in this book, some styles of country garden depend on flowers, for example, for their look (see p.108). But the use of plants ought to suit the feel you create, and that feel will be strongest and easiest to maintain if it is inspired by the ambience that your plot undoubtedly has. Design your ideal layout first without being distracted by the details of planting plans. Once you are sure of the overall concept you can progress to choosing the exact content of each planting area.

Profusion by a boundary wall (right) *At one time, the country garden would have been formally controlled to the very foot of grand boundary walls. Lesser means and regard for natural forms now allows a more relaxed approach.*

Twentieth-century styling (below) *The layout and use of elements has a modern feel but blends perfectly with the traditional buildings in this garden. Rampant climbers and gravel planting complete the setting.*

LOOKING FOR INSPIRATION

I can hear the horticulturally-minded reader thinking that the only ambience that many country plots have at the outset is the look of a disused farmyard, and the only way to cope with it is to dig and clip and tidy until it is transformed into an enclosure "fit" for horticultural

Style from existing structures *An outhouse and old carriage yard paved in granite setts, provide the inspiration for a country garden style of relaxed, muddled charm.*

display. But look at that untidy farmyard again and you might just see the potential of its charm and how it can be the perfect inspiration for your garden styling. That you cannot at first afford to have an old barn or modest farm structure demolished in your first flush of enthusiasm might just turn out to be the best thing you ever did for your garden. It could turn into the element that sets the style for the rest of your garden. Such an element will have the undoubted advantage of looking as though it

belongs and might well have a distressed charm that would otherwise take years to develop.

The worse place for inspiration is probably your local garden centre. Wandering around there for too long without a specific idea of your requirements is likely to result in an island bed of decorative conifers or heathers that completely belie their location. It is much better to spend your time walking or driving in your locality, soaking up the details of its charm that attract you, and assessing whether or not you might interpret them within your own boundaries. Visiting local craft fairs is also a good idea for they often encourage displays of traditional fieldcrafts that might be useful to you, including dry-stone walling, hurdle making and hedge laying. The results of such craftsmanship used within your plot might re-awaken a spirit of place you never imagined was there.

Styling the country garden then, is not simply a matter of decoration and details, it is also the conception of a plan and working with what you have to fulfil your requirements for country living.

Farmyard style *Some borrowed landscape across a paddock provides the backdrop to thatched outbuildings dripping with roses. This is not a "garden" in the accepted sense, but could it be improved?*

ENTRANCES AND EXITS

The mood of any particular country garden style is initiated by the main entrance, the dimensions of which nowadays are largely dictated by the width of your car. If seen against the house, the same styling as chosen for the house surrounds is appropriate for the entrance, harmonizing with the architectural style of the house. There is a balance to be struck between welcome and privacy when styling entrances, remembering that the most compelling entrances are a combination of structure and planting that tempts one to see what comes next.

Pedestrian entrances are most successful when treated as part of the incidental decoration of the garden and have most charm if their styling is understated and in complete harmony with planting as exemplified by the simple wooden gate opening on to a Berkshire garden, opposite. Next to it grows the large-leaved ivy, *Hedera colchica*.

Stone and brick archway *A heavy-looking archway such as this depends on surrounding planting for its softening effect.*

Classic iron gate *The beauty of a good iron gate is that it provides an effective barrier without impeding the view.*

Cottage garden gate *A white picket fence and matching gate is here suitably arched over with spring-flowering* Clematis montana.

Picket gates within an archway *Simple picket gates contrast with the grandeur of this brick-faced archway with iron decoration.*

Field gate *For many country property entrances, variations of the traditional five-bar gate are ideal.*

Stone arch *Planting balances the visual weight of this massive stone arch that serves as an inviting entrance to a Yorkshire garden.*

GARDEN WALLS

The walled garden (as part of a larger estate) for the protection of fruit and vegetables, a nursery garden or a pleasance, has medieval origins. The high, brick-built walls of such enclosures still exist and are one of the hallmarks of the traditional English country garden.

In a new plan, the expense of building walls can be prohibitive, but their value for linking buildings visually with elements of the garden, moulding space and strengthening character, is invaluable. Every type of wall has its own special charm, ranging from warm and friendly to tough and forbidding and, built in the vernacular style, a wall will forge a strong link between your garden and its surroundings. Every region has its local walling style or styles, based on available materials, whether clay (baked into many different types of brick) or stone. Brick walls are bonded with mortar, the modern version of which remains unaffected by the aerial roots of clinging plants, such as ivy. Dry-stone walling is an art that requires years of practice to perfect but can be learned by the enthusiastic amateur keen to make a good repair.

It is very difficult to justify removing an old wall—they are nearly always an immense asset visually, even in a next-to-ruinous state. No garden element creates privacy in quite the same way, nor provides a better foil to foliage.

Stone and brick *Reluctantly, one has to concede that a new wall would look bland compared with this lichen-rich mixture of dressed stone and bricks, laid without mortar.*

Lime-washed brick *A vine (Vitis sp.) and a simple, pelargonium-planted window-box are the perfect clothing for an old brick house wall, pierced by what was once an internal oven.*

Honey-colour stone *Mellowed stonework, such as in this house wall in Worcestershire, glows in the sunshine and complements the stems and blooms of old roses.*

Ancient dry-stone wall *With time, mosses and lichens will establish themselves in dry-stone walls. They have to be constructed of stone that splits in one direction, such as limestone or slate.*

Slate retaining wall *Slabs of slate, laid vertically, make a low retaining wall of sculptural beauty. Such details lend great character to gardens in areas where slate is quarried.*

Old brick *The brick elevations of walled gardens are the traditional support and shelter of fruit-bearing plants, including fruit tree cordons such as these, and* **espalier-trained** *specimens.*

Coursed flint work *In areas where chalk occurs naturally, flint walls are in order. This wall is faced with whole, rounded flints — sometimes they are split, or "knapped".*

FENCING AND HEDGING

Whereas walling has its place close to the house, and is ideal as a boundary within which to make a country fantasy in town, it is expensive and can make too definite a visual barrier between inside and out for the country location. Fencing or hedging are more appropriate. If you do need a new fence or hedge, or need to replace one, look to the local traditional types for both the right look and value for money. In many country locations, cleft chestnut or larch rails between oak posts are fairly common.

Some excellent zig-zag, pioneer-type timber stock fences were used in the United States before the advent of barbed wire. They consist of pairs of posts with each pair at 45 degrees to the next pair. The horizontal timbers are slotted between the pairs. Traditional woven sheep hurdles of willow or hazel, bound between stout cleft posts look excellent for five years or so, before they rot. Use them also for sheltering new plantations from the wind.

Timber fences need a wire netting or chain link backup to make them stock- and rabbit-proof. Chain link is more expensive but lasts longer—both are invisible at a distance. Bury the bottom edge of the wire 150 mm (6 in) deep, taking it up to the first horizontal on the post and rail fences and at least halfway up the hurdles.

Low, wrought or cast-iron railings have been used for a more sophisticated rural look since the eighteenth century, particularly in England and Ireland. Painted black, they too have the virtue of becoming totally invisible from a distance, since the horizontals are so thin.

Post-and-rail fencing *One of the beauties of traditional post-and-rail fencing, such as this three-rail example dividing a spring garden from sheep in the field beyond, is that you can see through it.*

As with timber fencing, wrought-iron railings can also be made rabbit-proof using wire netting.

HEDGING

It is a sad fact that many of the plants used to create a traditional type of hedge are not particularly fast growing, and it is for this reason that one sees so much *Chamaecyparis leylandii* used. But the visual effect of this straggling conifer in maturity has a devastating effect upon the countryside. Of native or naturalized plants, hawthorn (*Crataegus* spp.), blackthorn (*Prunus spinosa*) and field maple (*Acer campestre*) grow fastest though none are evergreen. Holly (*Ilex* spp.) makes an excellent impenetrable evergreen hedge. Gorse (*Ulex europaeus*), *Rosa rugosa* var. and beech (*Fagus sylvatica*) can also be used.

Fence and hedge combination *While the embryo hedge on this boundary establishes itself, a softwood post-and-rail fence serves as an attractive temporary division.*

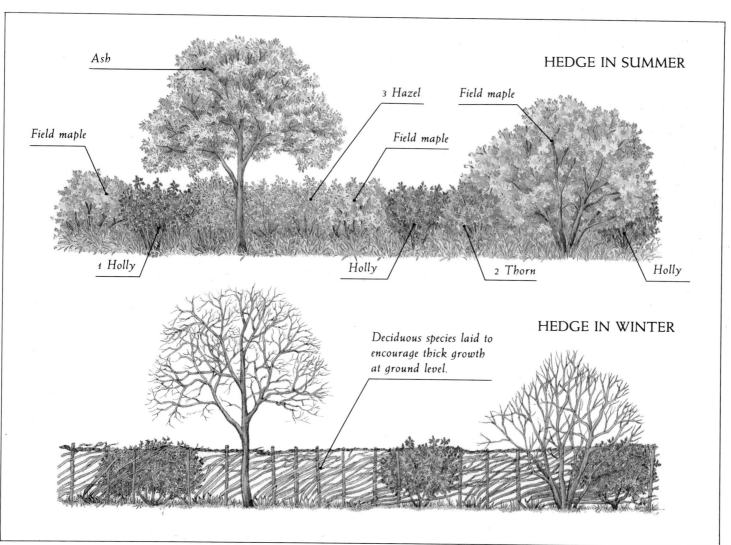

Ash

Field maple

3 Hazel

Field maple

Field maple

HEDGE IN SUMMER

1 Holly

Holly

2 Thorn

Holly

HEDGE IN WINTER

Deciduous species laid to encourage thick growth at ground level.

SURFACES AND LEVELS

The areas of a country garden closest to the house are made up of differing levels (comprising paths, terraces, yards and planting) interconnected by steps and/or ramps. When seen on plan, it is the correct proportion of these level areas, linked to the house, that should make a visually satisfying collage effect of interlocking shapes.

CHANGES OF LEVEL

Steps linking changes of level should be regarded more as a feature than a necessity and, if planned generously enough, become a series of landings that encourage leisurely perambulation. The landings lend themselves to decoration with planted pots and provide viewpoints.

Ideally, changes of level, which may well include some type of retaining wall, should be constructed either in the same material, or have some affinity to the surfacings of areas which they connect. Preferably, they should have a proportional relationship as well.

THE PROPORTIONS OF STEPS

The material of which the steps are made will, to a degree, dictate their proportions but, broadly speaking, step treads look well approximately 45 cm (18 ins) deep, with a riser of about 15 cm (6 ins). This allows an average pace as one goes up or down. Consider the function of riser and tread, depending on the dimensions and form of material you have chosen. Bricks on edge and stone make steps with crisp edges that will wear with time. Using some form of slab material makes it possible for the tread to overhang the risers, creating shadow and increasing sculptural form.

The form of the steps should be dictated by the garden layout. Steps designed within traditional, formal layouts tended to be centralized within the plan and comprise one grand flight. But for a more casual effect, steps may be staggered, they may turn on a landing or even have larger areas between the risers.

With the increasing use of heavy machinery to maintain the garden, steps can be a hazard to negotiate, and ramps become a necessary alternative. These are simpler, and therefore cheaper, to construct than steps, but they deserve just as much consideration as to their location and material of construction. If you plan to use a loose material, such as gravel, shingle or wood bark, the gradient of the ramp must be kept to a minimum or its surface will be washed away. A combination of shallow ramps with intermediate landings may be the solution. For heavy wear, consider using granite setts or engineering bricks set at an angle (haunched) in mortar over hardcore.

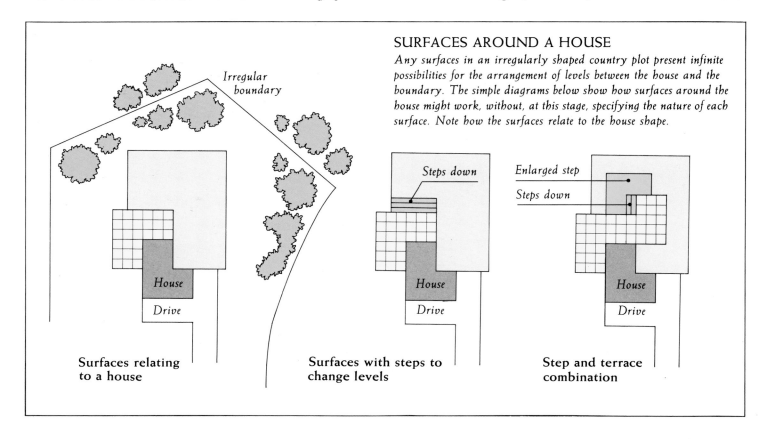

Irregular boundary

House

Drive

Surfaces relating to a house

SURFACES AROUND A HOUSE

Any surfaces in an irregularly shaped country plot present infinite possibilities for the arrangement of levels between the house and the boundary. The simple diagrams below show how surfaces around the house might work, without, at this stage, specifying the nature of each surface. Note how the surfaces relate to the house shape.

Steps down

House

Drive

Surfaces with steps to change levels

Enlarged step

Steps down

House

Drive

Step and terrace combination

Steps "au naturel" *In a landscape of rocky outcrops, such as the hard, granite face of Cornwall, what could be more appropriate than steps that resemble natural outcrops, engulfed by natural plant forms, including mosses, ferns and a variety of grasses?*

Worn stone steps *These beautifully simple steps have random stone treads that have become dished with the passing of countless feet. The steps link with a brick terrace punctuated with soil pockets that have allowed plants to self-seed, particularly* Alchemilla mollis.

Curved flight *Attention to the details of construction make this curved flight of steps both a useful pathway and an elegant garden feature. The treads are of slabs, with brick edging that links visually and physically with a stepped retaining wall.*

Shaped stone treads *The charm of this substantial flight of shaped stone steps in autumn, lies in the combination of hard material and random planting, including berberis and daisy flowers. The flight as a whole is more of a decorative feature than a useful path.*

CHANGES OF LEVEL

One of the great differences between a country plot and the suburban norm, is that country sites are often blessed with natural changes of level between one part of the garden and another. This might just be the gentle rise and fall associated with fertile lowlands, but it might be much more dramatic, including steep slopes and even rock outcrops. I say "blessed with" because many gardeners faced with billiard table flatness go to great lengths to create different levels for interest's sake, while others are unable to justify the upheaval and expense involved unless excavations are anyway required for new building or features such as ponds.

Whether man-made or natural in origin, there are two basic ways of manipulating changes of level to advantage. You either follow natural lines, making sure that any new slope or bank is contoured in a realistic way (see the garden plan on p.57), or you use the artifice of terracing, where flat areas are connected by banks, ramps or flights of steps. The two gardens below are examples of layouts where the whole character of the garden depends on the treatment of changes of level, including steps and terraces.

PRACTICALITIES

It is a very simple job for a surveyor to plot useful spot heights across your site, from a zero point such as your front door step. These points will help you to assess the number of steps of a particular height required to traverse a slope. Otherwise, take a tape and mark metre intervals from top to bottom of the slope. Then measure the vertical height from one point to a straight-edge held level (use a spirit-level) above it and projecting from the next metre mark up the slope. Duplicate the process for each of the metre marks and you can add up the total rise of the measured distance.

When undertaking any land shaping it is vital to ensure that topsoil remains on top. It should be removed and set aside before the subsoil layers are touched so that after moulding it can be replaced.

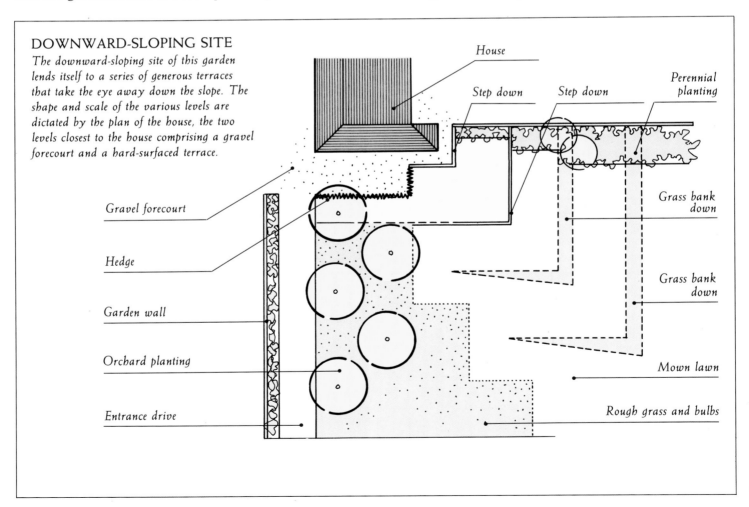

DOWNWARD-SLOPING SITE

The downward-sloping site of this garden lends itself to a series of generous terraces that take the eye away down the slope. The shape and scale of the various levels are dictated by the plan of the house, the two levels closest to the house comprising a gravel forecourt and a hard-surfaced terrace.

Gravel forecourt

Hedge

Garden wall

Orchard planting

Entrance drive

House

Step down

Step down

Perennial planting

Grass bank down

Grass bank down

Mown lawn

Rough grass and bulbs

The most common fault when planning changes of level is failing to achieve a balance of scale between the areas of the levels. Close to the house, terraces ought to relate to the area and shape of the house plan and should be generous enough to make a visual balance with it. Often they are too small and can never look anything but niggardly and out of proportion.

Interconnecting terraces often make for layouts of great interest and dynamism, leading the eye to the top or bottom of the terraced levels and towards views or prime features within the site. As with all garden design, get the pattern and shape of your layout right first, then worry about surfacing materials.

Any main pathway or year-round sitting area, particularly where there are steps, requires some form of hard surfacing in sympathy with the location. Otherwise the surfaces to choose from include turf (including rough grass as opposed to mown grass), groundcover plants, such as hypericum and spurge, cobbles and even larger fragments of rock. As a finishing touch there are a wide range of pots and other decorative features that can be positioned at various points to punctuate your plan.

UPWARD-SLOPING SITE

In this example, the house (with an adjacent barn) nestles beneath a rock face. The layout makes dramatic use of the upward-sloping site, including a grand flight of steps up to the highest point of the garden, and retaining walls shaped to match the dynamic plan.

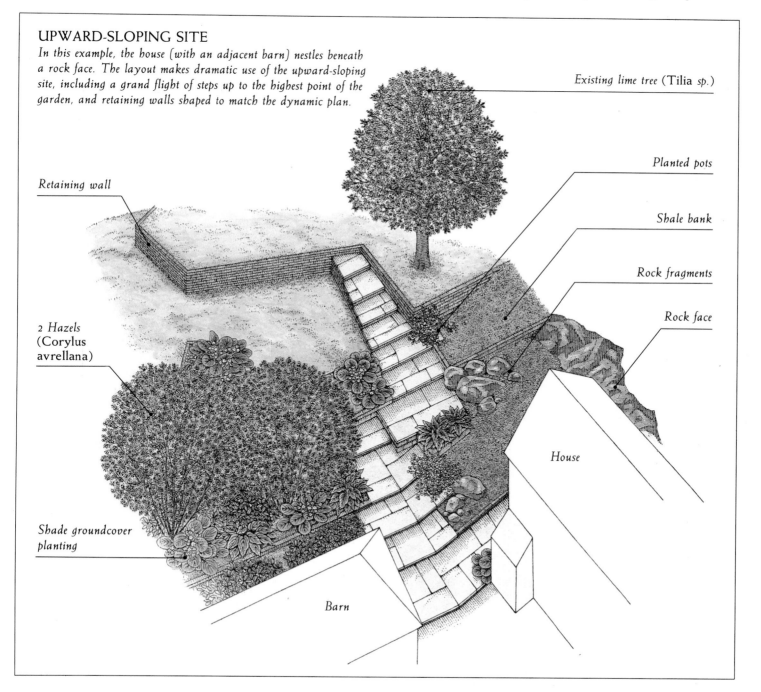

Existing lime tree (Tilia *sp.*)

Planted pots

Shale bank

Rock fragments

Rock face

Retaining wall

2 Hazels (Corylus avrellana)

House

Shade groundcover planting

Barn

PAVINGS

There are many diverse surface materials suitable for the pavings of a country garden, though physical criteria often make their selection impractical. Some surfacings, for instance, become slippery in winter; others pick up on damp boots and get carried indoors. Overriding these considerations, however, should be the visual fitness of the materials you choose for their context. Local stone, local gravel or local brick will never look inappropriate, and since it will not cost as much to transport them to you, they should be comparatively cheap. However, the major expense of paving is the cost of labour and, broadly speaking, the smaller the individual paving element the more expensive it will be to lay.

MIXING PAVINGS

Pavers, slightly larger than standard brick size, are being used more and more, but too much of this surfacing, like too much of any one surfacing, can appear too urban and slick for the country setting. Stone, on the other hand, is becoming more and more difficult to obtain. But what about mixing the materials to create a random, textured feel? Granite setts can be used in the mixture in granite areas, as can cobbles where they are available.

Pre-cast concrete paving slabs can be useful. Muted colours are better, but the chances are that a local firm making them will use the local stone as aggregate so their colour will blend with any existing structure. I prefer to use a textured slab whose pattern does not simulate stone.

JOINTING

The way in which jointing is completed makes an enormous difference to paving. It can be flush with the surface or given a trowelled slant, but neither technique looks as good as the joint being "rubbed back" slightly, that is, before the mortar of the joint sets hard, it is scraped away to just below the surface of the paving. The colour of the mortar joint should also be considered and altered if necessary (by choice of sand colour or by colour additive).

Planting in paving *Expanses of one type of paving will tend to look too urban in the country garden. A satisfying mix of paving types to adjoin a low stone wall can be made by combining random-sized, natural stone slabs with granite setts. The visual toughness of the stone is balanced by a planting of euphorbias and ivy.*

All the paving is laid on a consolidated base, but if you backfill the joints between the elements with topsoil, grass and self-seeders such as alchemilla will soften the look.

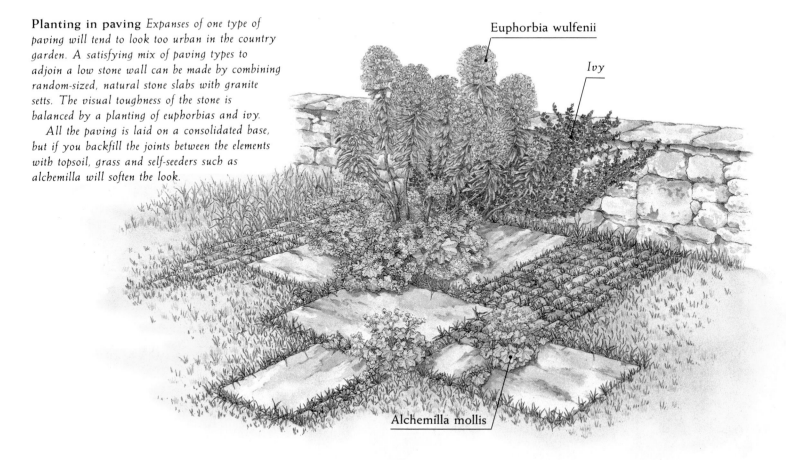

Euphorbia wulfenii

Ivy

Alchemilla mollis

Textured pre-cast slab *Pre-cast concrete paving slabs provide a sound, not-too-expensive surfacing material.*

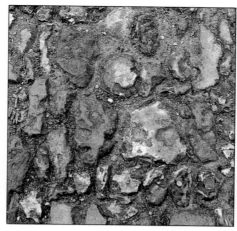

Random flints *This is a traditional paving type that looks marvellous with flint-faced buildings, but is time-consuming to lay.*

Stable tiles *These squares come in blocks of six, and were originally used in stables. They make a pleasant, small-scale pattern.*

Random stone paving *Laying random stone as well as this takes skill and time to ensure satisfying interlocking shapes.*

Distressed brick and stone *The charm of much country paving results from growth between the elements, such as this green moss.*

Brick and stone combination *A mixture of large and small paving elements can be very attractive, but requires careful planning.*

York stone slabs *Natural stone slabs produce a handsome, massively-scaled floor pattern. Plants will self-seed in the joints.*

Brick pavers *Specially hard, brick-sized pavers, or house bricks if they are sufficiently hard-baked, can be laid in many patterns.*

Simulated granite setts *Pre-cast concrete slabs that simulate granite setts can be remarkably attractive if well laid.*

GARDEN WALKS

Could you resist the allure of the walk shown opposite? Its shady, overgrown character seems irresistible and epitomizes the charm of the best garden walks, those that tempt you to explore, to see what is round the corner or at the end of the vista. It is the abundance of greenery on either side of a walk that gives it its particular allure while other features can be an added bonus. The large mossy rock beside the walk opposite appears to be strategically placed to encourage the passer-by to stop, sit and wonder at the beauty of the surroundings. Such a path is not a main route through the garden, it is an incident within the total, styled to suit its particular site.

Between buildings *A garden walk between buildings can be very tempting. Here the distant viewpoint is a strong attraction, as is the expectation of views around corners.*

Towards woodland *A planting of astilbe lines one side of this gravelled garden walk that disappears into woodland.* **Rubus tricolor** *provides groundcover on the left.*

Behind a building *A pollarded tree trunk and an old cask used as a water butt furnish this concrete-surfaced walk that disappears behind an old timber-faced building.*

Between clipped box *This gravel walk edged with stone tiles, in a New England-type garden, has a formal charm. Box-edged beds filled with herbs, demand closer attention.*

Through abundant planting *Old roses, alchemilla and a globe artichoke with handsome grey leaves line a romantic gravel path that leads to a flower garden.*

Beneath trained fruit trees *Fruit trees trained over frames force the view down this path. The style is architectural suggesting a complex network of paths to explore.*

GARDEN BUILDINGS

If your house has not set the style of your country garden, its outbuildings may; for one of the great virtues of older houses in the country is that they are often accompanied by a barn, or an old coach house, a bothy, a shed or even a pigsty. All can be used as features in a layout, while the form of such a structure will give clues to the sort of materials you might use elsewhere in the garden. Defunct farm shelters are sometimes a bonus as they might provide a sheltered courtyard that can be gravelled.

Always consider a change of use for a structure that might at first seem outmoded, especially if it was originally built in the same style as the house and on a suitable scale. Nothing would be more inappropriate, for example, than to remove a traditional shelter, and then to turn to a catalogue of pre-fabricated garages, when, with a little thought, the original would have served your car admirably and have blended perfectly visually.

It is very easy to be tempted by advertisements offering "period" conservatories and other garden buildings. Although some of these offer a credible match to some styles of building, if available in the right scale, many are over-ornamented with decorative details that are a parody of the original model. The country home and garden deserves much simpler, more practical structures.

Some modern outbuildings now have considerable character. Not the garden-centre cedar wood shed, which

Converted stabling *Old brick and tile loose boxes have been skilfully worked into the layout of this garden, for use as storage units. Planting and tubs turn the structure into a handsome addition to the garden.*

is still far too "thin" and lacking in substance for a country garden feature, but new timber stabling and loose boxes or dog runs, which can look well-proportioned, stocky and practical, despite their newness.

One of the problems of siting and using small buildings within a layout is their scale—their ground plan is often too small for their height, and they easily become a pimple on the plot. Where they are absolutely necessary, it is a good idea to attach such a building to another structure to bulk up the overall feel.

DECORATIVE QUALITIES VERSUS PRACTICALITY

The type of building that you have in a garden might be either decorative or practical; if the latter, your planting can improve it. It pays to remember, however, that the purely decorative eye-catching building quickly becomes a liability, since its maintenance is so high. Unless extremely well built, deterioration of such buildings soon

sets in due to their lying unused for long periods, especially through winter dampness. Furthermore, such a building can all too easily become a secondary store, a glory hole for mowers, redundant garden furniture, or last summer's barbecue. Such usage will soon remove any decorative qualities that the building had.

The more practical garden building can be designed or converted to provide specific storage areas, including tool sheds and such like, to meet the increasing demand for adequate, secure storage in country gardens. The charm of such buildings will lie in their functional structure, how comfortably they fit into the garden layout, the paved approach to them and their complementary associated planting, as you will see on page 51.

Focal point of a garden *A splendid tower was designed as the focal point of this stylish garden. It provides a usable store at ground level and studio/office space with a fine view, above.*

BUILDINGS AND PLANTS

One of the joys of the natural-looking garden is the way rampant but controlled plant growth modifies the look of buildings. A structure can be transformed by the softening influence of plants that will clothe walls. They might grow up against it (like ceanothus), grow on supports fixed to the wall (either twining like jasmine or tied in like a rambling rose), or cling by means of aerial roots (like ivy).

Although ivies and evergreen honeysuckle are indispensable for their year-round contribution, most dramatic in their seasoned visual impact on a building are deciduous climbers that grow up quickly through spring and summer. The hop, for example (*Humulus lupulus*), will scramble up and over a building and bear attractive fruit clusters at an astonishing rate, before dying back as winter approaches. Prior to planting, construct a substantial network of wires against the wall to support the climber.

CONSERVATORIES

The classic meeting of building and plants, however, is in the conservatory, or glasshouse. There has been a revival of interest in the conservatory recently, fired by the manufacture of glazed units designed to provide both a home-extension and a place in which to grow plants.

The "clothed" building *A deciduous climber, such as this hop, will transform a building during its growing season. As such a plant dies back, make sure you remove all old growth from roof tiles, gutters and other important structural elements of a building.*

These two functions are difficult to combine, however, for conservatory plants need copious amounts of water, including spraying—requirements that do not mix with indoor furnishings. A small glazed extension can suffer from extreme fluctuations of temperature. Sited to catch the sun's rays, it will become too hot for plants in mid-summer and may become surprisingly cold at night.

Traditionally, the conservatory is a larger building, kept separate from the general living area. It might indeed be free-standing, a stroll away from the garden doors of the house. It is a place in which to brighten the dull days of late winter (for those of us in the chillier temperate zones) and to enjoy the fragrance and colour of tender, or out-of-season blooms. Its size makes fluctuations of temperature less extreme and easier to control.

Building a new conservatory along traditional lines involves major expense, but you might be lucky enough to inherit one that will respond to a little judicious renovation. Then you will have to decide whether to heat it or not, remembering that to warm a single-glazed house to even modest temperatures is an expensive business. Without heat, it is still possible to bring on early spring and summer flowers with great success.

PAVILIONS

If you free yourself from the task of keeping an exotic plant collection, your requirements for a garden building are less exacting and you might settle for a structure with large glazed areas in the elevations (so that you can use it partly as a greenhouse), but with a traditional roof of tiles, slates or shingles. Such a structure might be called a pavilion (for want of a better term) and will be most successful if it can fulfil a practical function, providing shelter or shade near a terrace, for example.

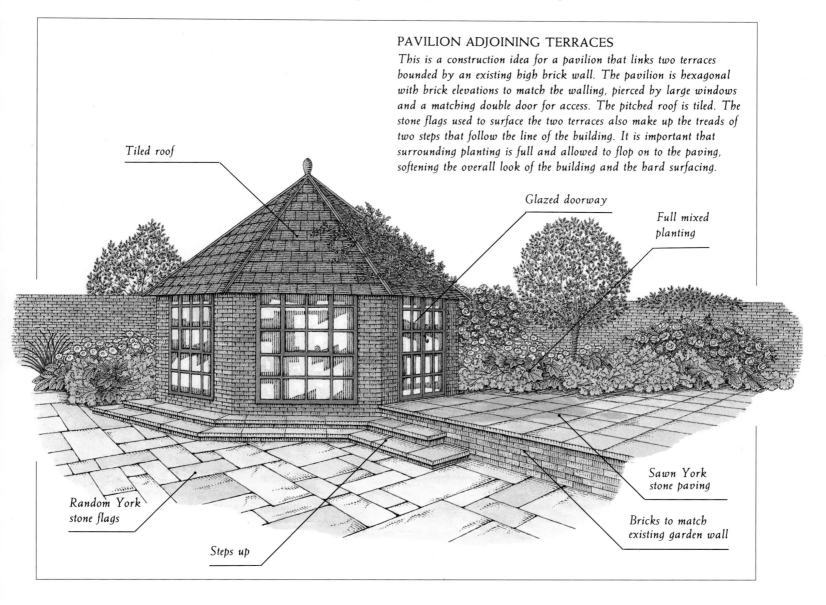

PAVILION ADJOINING TERRACES

This is a construction idea for a pavilion that links two terraces bounded by an existing high brick wall. The pavilion is hexagonal with brick elevations to match the walling, pierced by large windows and a matching double door for access. The pitched roof is tiled. The stone flags used to surface the two terraces also make up the treads of two steps that follow the line of the building. It is important that surrounding planting is full and allowed to flop on to the paving, softening the overall look of the building and the hard surfacing.

Tiled roof

Glazed doorway

Full mixed planting

Random York stone flags

Steps up

Sawn York stone paving

Bricks to match existing garden wall

THE GARDEN IN WINTER

I think every winter is more beautiful than the last. From a gardener's point of view there is satisfaction in the "put to bed" look of early winter—with leaves finally raked, bonfires burned and farmyard manure spread. Shapes are strong in the garden at this time of the year too—shapes of lawns and shapes of paths, and the strong shapes of evergreens that come into their own as their deciduous neighbours are reduced to skeletons. I love the black look of yew (*Taxus* sp.), and, if the winter is mild, the green of early hellebores with the pale yellow of winter jasmine seen against them.

The pleasures of a winter garden are generally subtle however—no banks of colour here, but what pleasure from the earliest snowdrops and aconites, and the first waves of scent from the winter honeysuckle (*Lonicera fragrantissima*), sarcococca and hamamelis. Sharp frosty mornings invigorate, and there is always a clear conscience about garden chores. It is time for a country walk to soak in the neat black and white look that stretches out from your garden to the landscape beyond, for at no time of year does the garden blend better with its backdrop. Now is the time to study the natural contours that surround your garden. Sloping ground beyond your boundaries will establish a rhythm where the ridges of slopes intersect—a rhythm that you might interpret in the pattern of your layout.

After snow there's a further magic. The small detail is hidden and only large, broad shapes register. If the proportions of your garden look well in mid-winter, with shrub masses working in scale with their backdrop, then your garden will only improve during the luxuriant, growing months of spring and summer.

Delights (right) *Late winter's compensations include the blooms of giant snowdrops* (Galanthus elwesii) *and* Helleborus corsicus, *with the marbled leaves of* Arum italicum 'Marmoratum'.

Garden in a winter landscape (left) *Evergreen shapes show up well in the stark winter landscape, in this case yew* (Taxus baccata), *and monkey puzzles* (Araucaria araucana).

WINTER FLOWERS

There is a quiet, delicate beauty to winter's flowers. They are usually of pale colours, particularly soft greens, and many are highly scented. This array was cut from my garden in southern England in December, after an unusually mild start to winter. Winter blooms do not form flamboyant displays but are gems to discover when much of the garden lies dormant and strong foliage shapes are centre stage.

Cyclamen *A hardy variety, the brave blooms of which have a delicious fragrance*

Viburnum fragrans *A deciduous viburnum but produces scented florets well into winter*

Cupressus arizonica 'Conica' *Produces a sea of tiny yellow flowers*

Viburnum tinus (left) *Evergreen, with eye-catching florets throughout winter*

Rosemary (Rosmarinus officinalis fastigiatus) *Light frosts allow rosemary flowers to survive*

Autumn-flowering cherry (Prunus subhirtella 'Autumnalis')

Ivy (Hedera helix) *Ivy flowers are often ignored but have a graphic quality*

Winter jasmine (Jasminium nudiflorum) *Flowers unfailingly on bare stems*

Euphorbia wulfenii *Tenacious, green flowerheads are a winter-time bonus*

Mahonia japonica *The scented racemes of this shrub complement its striking leaf shape*

CASE TWO—THE SURVEY

The large garden, right, had its prime views blocked by hedging, a mixed border, and an unnatural mound made from the spoil from a pond excavation. The pond was separated from the main bulk of the garden and the house surrounds needed rationalizing.

THE REVISED PLAN

In the proposed new garden the spoil from the pond excavations is contoured into more naturalistic shapes, and added to by the spoil from a certain amount of re-shaping of the pool. The central hedge and mixed border have been removed to open up the required views.

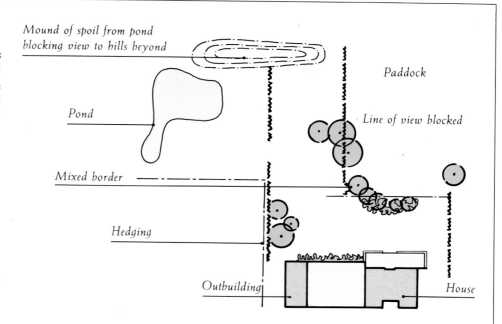

Mound of spoil from pond blocking view to hills beyond

Paddock

Pond

Line of view blocked

Mixed border

Hedging

Outbuilding

House

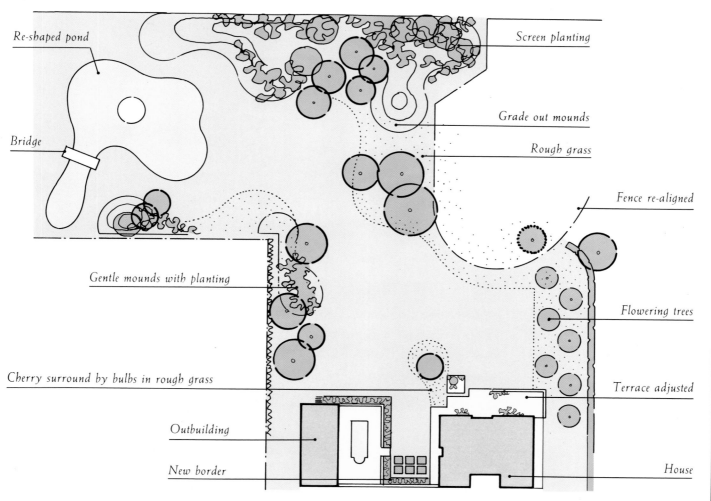

Re-shaped pond

Screen planting

Bridge

Grade out mounds

Rough grass

Fence re-aligned

Gentle mounds with planting

Flowering trees

Cherry surround by bulbs in rough grass

Terrace adjusted

Outbuilding

New border

House

STEMS IN WINTER

One of the most subtle, but nevertheless pleasurable joys of the country garden in winter, is the abundance of colors and textures displayed by branches and stems denuded of their foliage. This selection was taken from my own garden during a stroll in winter sunshine, when the angle of sunlight was low enough to highlight bark patterns, luminous stems, graphic spikes and downy twigs.

Bamboo (Arundinaria viridistriata)
Remarkably delicate canes with buff stem-sheaths

Winged euonymus (Euonymus alatus)
Partially ribbed stems are a bonus after brilliant autumnal leaf color

Salix fargesii *A stout, densely-green stem that will turn to a deep, shining brown*

Violet willow (Salix daphnoides)
A young shoot still covered in its downy bloom

Dogwood (Cornus alba 'Sibirica') *Fresh, vigorous growth has the brightest red color*

Snow gum (Eucalyptus niphophila)
"Bleached" bark flake from one of the most beautiful of gums

Stag's horn sumach (Rhus typhina) *Has a texture reminiscent of the velvet covering a stag's antlers*

Cider gum (Eucalyptus gunnii) *Bark flake naturally curled to reveal deep orange*

Stephanandra tanakae *The sepia tint of stephanandra's stems is a winter bonus*

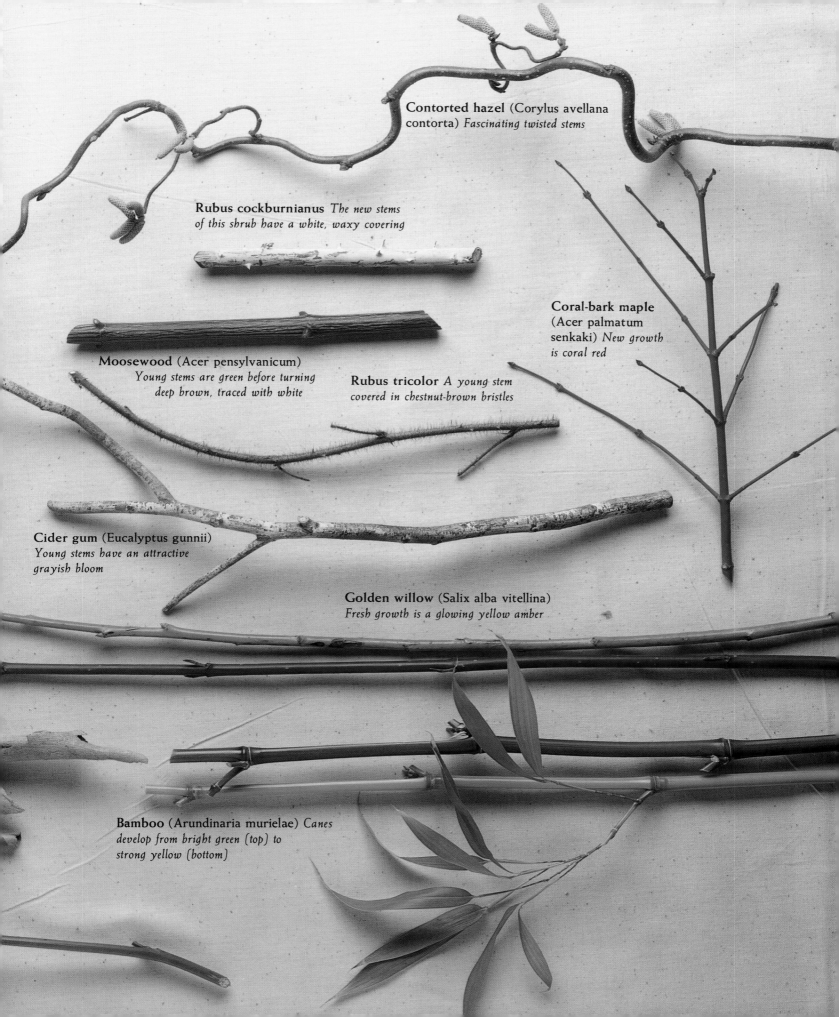

Contorted hazel (Corylus avellana contorta) *Fascinating twisted stems*

Rubus cockburnianus *The new stems of this shrub have a white, waxy covering*

Coral-bark maple (Acer palmatum senkaki) *New growth is coral red*

Moosewood (Acer pensylvanicum) *Young stems are green before turning deep brown, traced with white*

Rubus tricolor *A young stem covered in chestnut-brown bristles*

Cider gum (Eucalyptus gunnii) *Young stems have an attractive grayish bloom*

Golden willow (Salix alba vitellina) *Fresh growth is a glowing yellow amber*

Bamboo (Arundinaria murielae) *Canes develop from bright green (top) to strong yellow (bottom)*

HOPEFUL SIGNS

Shelley's line, "If Winter comes, can Spring be far behind?", has a particular significance in the country garden. Depending on the severity of the season and the aspect of your site, there will be signs of new growth long before the official end of winter. As soon as sunshine brings the most fragile warmth to sheltered spots, the first shoots start to appear, followed by the earliest flowers of the year. Few leaves are brave enough to show, since sharp frosts are still about, but aconites and snowdrops are made of sterner stuff and show their cheering, defiant blooms even as the last snows are melting. They are followed by the first *Iris stylosa*, by species crocus and that annual wonder, the early-flowering *Narcissus* 'February Gold'. In wild boggy areas there are banks of butterbur (*Petasites hybridus*), with its felty leaves, and in woodland the first shoots of dog's mercury (*Mercurialis perennis*), with hazel (*Corylus* sp.) catkins and pussy willow (*Salix* sp.) Like the first stirrings of a hibernating mammal, the annual natural cycle is bringing the garden slowly back to life.

Naturalized snowdrops (right) *A bank of both single and double forms of snowdrop (*Galanthus nivalis*) is one of the most cheering sights of late winter, here shown with narcissus pushing through.*

Winter aconites (below) *Another winter beauty, the winter aconite (*Eranthis hyemalis*), naturalizes itself in bold drifts. The flowers open in sunshine to produce sheets of deep buttercup-yellow flowers.*

WINTER VEGETABLES

There is nothing like fresh vegetables to preserve the spirits through winter. Leeks, the *Brassica* crops and Swiss chard are plants of architectural beauty while growing, as well as providing ingredients for warming dishes. Root and tubers are worthwhile if you have the time and space.

Spinach (Spinacia oleracea) *Sow smooth-seeded varieties throughout winter*

Brussels sprout (Brassica oleracea gemnifera) *After frost, sprouts are the tastiest of brassicas*

Parsnip (Pastinaca sativa) *A delicious root that is completely frost hardy*

Leek (Allium ampeloprasum) *A stalwart stem for fresh flavour when all else fails*

Turnip (Brassica rapa) *Less hardy than swede but some varieties have edible foliage*

Swede (Brassica napus) *A versatile root that can be left growing until required*

Red Cabbage (Brassica oleracea) *A colourful addition to stews and winter salads*

Perpetual spinach *Mid-summer sowing will provide a succulent winter crop*

Celery (Apium graveolens) *For soups and braising as well as winter salads*

Main-crop Potato (Solanum tuberosum)

Swiss chard (Beta vulgaris) *Use the stems like celery and the leaves like spinach*

Savoy cabbage (Brassica oleracea balluta) *A heart warming, old friend of a vegetable that looks so well growing*

Cauliflower (Brassica oleracea) *Slower-maturing main crop varieties will last into winter*

THE NATURAL GARDEN

It can be said that all gardens are natural to an extent. But we saw earlier (on pages 14 and 15) how, through different periods of history, styling and layout were decidedly unnatural, in that the plants they contained were restricted and clipped to fit into a classical, formalized ground pattern. Even in the eighteenth century, when styling was much softer, the "landscaped" look was supposed to create an idealized version of nature on a scale where the horticultural element was no smaller than the tree—again hardly natural.

Only in the latter half of the twentieth century, with all the horticultural input of the nineteenth and early twentieth centuries behind us, do we find ourselves re-assessing our situation more practically and considering a new form of garden style, which I shall call the natural garden. Such a style is essentially rural, although elements of it can of course be re-interpreted in an urban location. It is carefully designed to serve the family that uses it, having significant portions in which costly maintenance is minimal. The planting style is relaxed in appearance and, being partly derived from indigenous vegetation, is attractive to native fauna. It is constructed (as far as possible) in the idiom of the structure it surrounds and mindful of styles beyond its boundaries, so that, as a whole, the garden is a welcome addition to its locality rather than a horticulturalized embarrassment. Some tradition-alists might be shocked at the absence of weed-free earth, edged and stripped lawns, manicured, mop-headed trees, and blasts of annual colour in the natural garden. If they look a second time, however, they will find a garden at peace with its landscape, alive with softer pleasures and, in its midst, a relaxed and happy gardener.

Careful detailing
Natural garden style calls for relaxed, almost haphazard-looking detailing that is in fact carefully planned. The two voluptuous examples shown here include: a simple, unpainted garden bench (right), couched amongst the delicate, nodding heads of quaking-grass, species gladioli and a grouping of ferns, and foreground anaphalis (left) with pink towering spikes of digitalis.

NATURAL PLANTING

The natural garden look depends greatly on its planting style. It should broadly follow the zone system discussed on page 28, with the more alien species planted in the shelter of the house and/or outbuildings, then a central transitional zone, before there is a blending of plants with native species beyond the boundary.

PLANTING SCALE

The scale of the plants you use should also alter with zone. When adjacent to any structure, plant scale should relate to it, but be generally small including specimens with some architectural form to tie in with the form of the building. Most, however, should provide a considered profusion that softens the look of the structure.

In the boundary zone, on the other hand, masses of the more native species should be in scale with their backdrop, bold swathes in sympathy with distant woods, a hillside or a chequered field pattern. And in between these, in the intermediate zone, a subtle transition.

Looking at the examples of natural garden planting on these pages, it may be difficult to imagine the jump from theory to practice when it comes to achieving that rampant look. The answer is to develop the planting technique that I call "drift and flow" (see p.68). It approximates the naturally-occurring effect of plant drifts and will create the relaxed, (some call it "weedy") look, ideal for the natural garden.

The successful natural-style country gardener comes to understand the plants he or she uses, noting their rates of growth, how they reproduce and how successful they are at it. It then becomes clear that some plants can be left to grow and multiply willy-nilly without the fear of total invasion, while others, those with vigorous root systems, need equally vigorous cutting back and root restriction.

Soft jungle of forms (right) *Verbascum, fennel and digitalis, in the foreground, mixed casually with alchemilla, lavender and evening primrose beyond, are here established in gravel.*

Garden incorporated with the countryside *The harmony between decorative planting and transitional planting between the garden building, the duck pond and the field beyond, epitomizes natural style in this garden.*

DRIFT AND FLOW EFFECT

The drift and flow effect of planted masses starts out in a far from casual way. Once established it will of course fill out, and to a degree alter, since the perennial groups get broader and the bienniels self-seed and come up unexpectedly. But the range of plants that you wish to grow has to be planted out and established, including a skeleton framework of shrubby material. It is this skeleton grouping that prevents the effect from becoming a mess and continues to provide form and interest through the winter when much perennial material will have died down.

You now work down in scale, choosing perennials, biennials and finally annuals, starting with those plants that have the strongest forms. For a plant's form (its overall growth, shape, and the texture of its leaves) is with you far

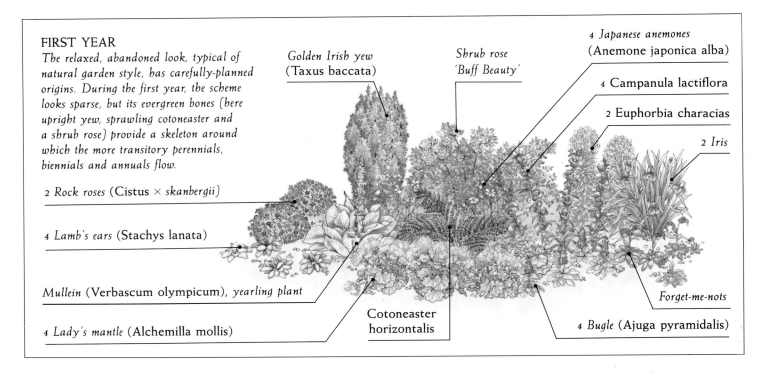

FIRST YEAR
The relaxed, abandoned look, typical of natural garden style, has carefully-planned origins. During the first year, the scheme looks sparse, but its evergreen bones (here upright yew, sprawling cotoneaster and a shrub rose) provide a skeleton around which the more transitory perennials, biennials and annuals flow.

2 Rock roses (Cistus × skanbergii)

4 Lamb's ears (Stachys lanata)

Mullein (Verbascum olympicum), *yearling plant*

4 Lady's mantle (Alchemilla mollis)

Golden Irish yew (Taxus baccata)

Shrub rose 'Buff Beauty'

4 Japanese anemones (Anemone japonica alba)

4 Campanula lactiflora

2 Euphorbia characias

2 Iris

Forget-me-nots

Cotoneaster horizontalis

4 Bugle (Ajuga pyramidalis)

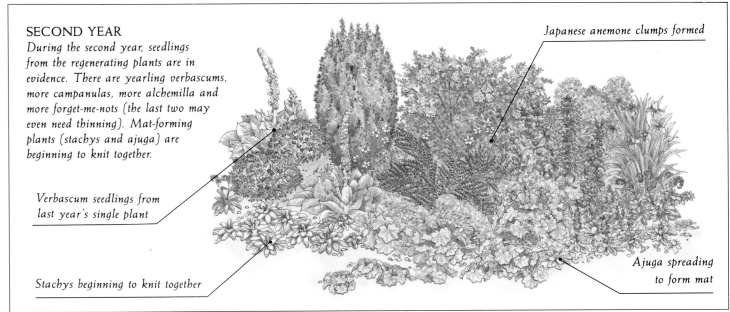

SECOND YEAR
During the second year, seedlings from the regenerating plants are in evidence. There are yearling verbascums, more campanulas, more alchemilla and more forget-me-nots (the last two may even need thinning). Mat-forming plants (stachys and ajuga) are beginning to knit together.

Verbascum seedlings from last year's single plant

Stachys beginning to knit together

Japanese anemone clumps formed

Ajuga spreading to form mat

longer than its flower colour. This is not to say that at the back of your mind you are not thinking about an eventual colour range *as well*.

Plot your selected plants on paper, envisaging in your mind's eye the finished effect in elevation while drawing it in plan. Use groups of plants (some people only work with odd numbers, but I don't think it matters), drifting a group of six or seven of this with three or five of that. Allow each plant enough space to grow to its preferred size, starting with the large things and working down to the small.

There are two further rules: firstly, select plants from commercial catalogues only (the plant dictionaries are excellent too, but to be practical they must be used in conjunction with listings that represent a real source); and secondly, when you think you have finished your plan, take out half the types of plant you had first considered and double up on the number of the remaining types. We all use too much variety, weakening the visual impact of each plant type by planting too few specimens and providing them with too much competition.

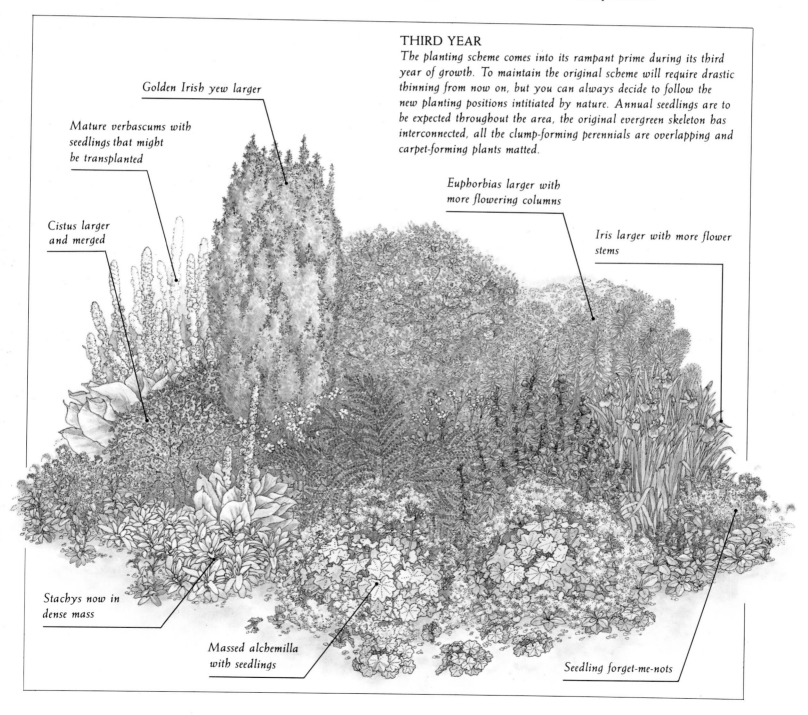

THIRD YEAR

The planting scheme comes into its rampant prime during its third year of growth. To maintain the original scheme will require drastic thinning from now on, but you can always decide to follow the new planting positions intitiated by nature. Annual seedlings are to be expected throughout the area, the original evergreen skeleton has interconnected, all the clump-forming perennials are overlapping and carpet-forming plants matted.

Golden Irish yew larger

Mature verbascums with seedlings that might be transplanted

Cistus larger and merged

Euphorbias larger with more flowering columns

Iris larger with more flower stems

Stachys now in dense mass

Massed alchemilla with seedlings

Seedling forget-me-nots

NEGLECTED CORNERS

We all tend to be too sophisticated in our plant selections. A good source of ideas for more natural plant groups, if not nature herself, is a good and preferably neglected rubbish dump. One longs to see behind the garden door of a manicured period garden to those areas left for compost, sweepings and prunings, to see what has grown of its own accord and what its neighbour might be. The neglected corners of an old garden are often full of incidental plant associations. Sometimes they overlay a previous conscious planting design. To a degree, such natural accidents are the charm of the "olde worlde" garden, but conscious efforts to achieve the same look can be too clever by half. The accidents are an inevitable feature of the natural country garden and can be regarded as a delightful visual bonus. But if you wish to recreate such "accidental" plant groupings, look at the examples below for ideas.

Natural-looking association *A purple-leaved vine (*Vitis vinifera purpurea*), creeps up a dead tree trunk, and through it a clematis has established itself to make a wonderfully decorative association.*

Forgotten niche *The perennial sweet pea (Lathyrus latifolius) frames an unconscious grouping of potted house-leeks (Sempervivum sp) with a climbing rose and clematis foliage.*

Neglected outhouse *A pink clematis has associated itself with variegated ivy, and a sheet of blue campanula, heuchera leaves and a fern, all against a sandstone wall.*

Around a water butt *An old, brimming water butt and down spout forms a dilapidated, but charming, support for a rambling, pink-flowering clematis.*

Defunct workings *Racemes of purple wisteria frame the stone sluice support above an old, and now defunct, weir stop-cock. If you are lucky enough to have such an incidental feature in your garden, its visual attributes will only increase as plants grow around it.*

DISTRESSING TECHNIQUES

The techniques for creating the soft, old-established look that epitomizes the natural garden might be termed distressing, in the same way that there are decorating techniques, using paint for example, to distress walls or woodwork. In the garden, the aim is to soften newly-built or hard-looking surfaces and structures using plant material.

The natural garden design should allow for full and luxuriant planting in association with buildings and paving. It is a good idea to establish an architecturally striking plant as a feature of this planting. Acanthus and euphorbias are particular favourites of mine for this role.

TECHNIQUES FOR PAVING
There are various sources of inspiration for the distressed look as far as paving is concerned. The effect of moss on stone in permanently damp areas is wonderful, but potentially lethal if allowed to develop across paving used as a thoroughfare. Neglected paved yards become overrun in a multitude of attractive ways. Aspects of these looks can be achieved in a conscious ground plan that allows for grass growing between slabs or sets; you can use a hover mower to occasionally trim the grass and so control the look (see p.41).

Many gardeners try to achieve the look by planting alpines through paving, but if the mass of plants is too varied and unnatural in its placement, it creates an

Using plant associations You can achieve a distressed look by introducing unexpected combinations. Here annual cosmos is seen with the huge glaucous leaves of one of the kale family between a shrub rose and a conifer.

SHORT CUTS TO RUIN
Plants in unusual places *The distressed look is based on the softening visual effect that plants have on buildings and paving. Look around you and you will see all kinds of examples of plants colonizing man-made structures. House-leeks (Sempervivum Sp.) establish themselves in the most unlikely of places. Where stone is used as a roofing material, for example, they will make attractive outcrops across a shaded roof. You can simulate this natural effect by establishing house-leeks in a simple wire-netting basket, lined with sphagnum moss and filled with a half-and-half mix of soil-based compost and grit. Attach wires and secure the basket by hooking them under convenient tiles.*

Wall folly *You can even build your own ruined pile if you are committed to the distressed look! Use a few second-hand, local bricks to build a section of walling, saving broken ones to make a crumbling edge. Render the lower courses, leaving a jagged upper edge (you can always hack this away if you are not satisfied with the degree of ruin). Leave for a week, then paint all the surfaces with well-rotted manure solution. Fill any crevice or revealed frog (the hollow of a brick, not the croaking sort) with a little soil-based compost, and then plant with stonecrops.*

unsettling and spotty effect. A visually stronger effect can be achieved by sticking entirely to aubretia or *Polygonum vaccinifolium*.

TECHNIQUES FOR WALLS AND ROOFS

Vertical surfaces can be distressed as well, most simply by choosing the right climbing plants—native ivies, honeysuckles, hops, vines, or the beautiful climbing *Hydrangea petiolaris* (for a shady location)—and providing complementary supports.

On a smaller scale, however, plants can be introduced between the stones or bricks of a wall. Wallflowers prefer such a location, while forms of campanula and the little pink perennial erigeron can be grown in this way.

The secret of success is to be able to sustain the correct amount of moisture in the wall. Many old walls were built without a dampproof course and, depending on the porosity of their brick or stone, took up water from the earth like blotting paper; they will sustain plant material. Old brick walls will probably have been built using lime mortar which, being softer than modern cement mortar, is a medium in which seedlings will establish themselves—albeit to the ultimate detriment of the wall.

With new walls, you must either choose a method of construction that allows moisture into the structure, such as dry-stone walling, or build-in planting pockets where a little peat will retain moisture. Double-thickness brick wall construction lends itself to having the gap between the two thicknesses of bricks filled with a peat-based mixture.

Where damp walls are undesirable you can resort to attaching containers to the surface of the wall. In areas where stone is used for roofing, house-leeks (*Sempervivum* sp.) are a natural feature, clinging precariously to crevices. To establish such a group artificially, wire a small netting planter (as shown on page 72) to a shady part of the roof, plant small house-leeks in it, and keep it moist.

Much of the charm of old-established country buildings results from lichen and moss growth on walls and roofs. It can be encouraged prematurely by painting new stone, brick or tiles with diluted cow manure or a solution of milk, but you will have to suffer the temporary smell!

A sense of forgotten romance (left) *Natural garden styling can convey a strong sense of lost romance. Here an inviting doorway is flanked by a bank of white honesty and a carpet of herbaceous geraniums.*

Rambling charm (above right) *Shade-tolerant blue cranesbill (Geranium 'Johnson's Blue') grows in a haphazard way beneath orchard fruit trees in a charming natural garden.*

Incidental feature (below right) *Are the rocks just a visual pleasure or a seat in this Kentish garden? They are both and, couched in a mixed planting, provide an unconscious sculptural feature.*

THE RUGGED GARDEN

Within the overall concept of the natural country garden look there are subdivisions that are styled by the conditions imposed by specific locations. One of these is the coast, where many country gardeners battle not only with winds, but with salt-laden ones that sculpt every element of their garden and create a rugged beauty. Here you must use plants that will tolerate blown salt and sand, such as euonymus and elaeagnus, with thrift (*Armeria maritima*), or sea buckthorn (*Hippophae rhamnoides*).

GROUND-HUGGING FORMS

On marginal farming land or moorland there is another rugged look that is inspired by natural rock that might occur within gardens. As on the coast, the wind will often have shaped the land forms, giving trees a characteristic look and rounding the masses of heather or gorse until they too look like rocks. Other plant species native to this kind of dramatic location will have developed a ground-hugging form, growing in carpeting clumps, such as blueberry (*Vaccinium* sp:).

CLIMATIC EFFECTS

It is not just the wind that moulds the rugged garden, for the associated temperature is all-important. Native coniferous vegetation, heathers and gorses (*Ulex* sp.) have adapted to rugged garden locations where the cold can be intense. Warmer wind-blown areas support other plants with leaf adaptations, such as broom (*Cytisus* sp.), while the oil content of many herbs is an adaptation originally developed as a protection against the doubly drying combination of sun and wind.

Rounded forms (right) *Wind has rounded the rocks, a hardy sycamore* (Acer pseudoplatanus), *and a fleshy-leaved* Griselinia littoralis *in a rugged coastal garden.*

Craggy pines (left) *Pine trees make excellent wind breaks, becoming craggy and rugged with age. These sculptural tree trunks are of the Monterey pine* (Pinus radiata).

There are many subtleties to the rugged garden by the sea. Within sheltered valleys running down to the sea, the wind-rounded forms that are such a striking feature of exposed coastal gardens give way to an exciting range of plants, including daisy bush (*Olearia* sp.) and the many forms of pittosporum and even fuchsias. These more decorative plants will thrive in the intensity of light reflected from the sea and benefit from the frost-free pocket that will probably exist there.

Other coastal locations, often a little further inland, or on an estuary, are part of a plain that stretches flat to the sea. They suffer the buffeting of salt-laden winds and give the impression of being *on* their landscape, rather than *in* it. The scale of sky and sea demand a tough garden style.

CREATING SHELTER

In any rugged location where salt wind is a problem that reduces your enjoyment of the garden and young plant growth, the most practical and the best visual solution is to plant a belt of native trees and/or shrubs for shelter.

Look to those plants that thrive nearby and would provide a wind break, including tall grasses. Conifers that thrive in maritime and moorland conditions, including Corsican pine, are particularly useful, as are the tough, beautiful thorns (*Crataegus* sp.) and evergreen holm oak (*Quercus ilex*). If the site is very exposed it is probably not worth considering too much decorative planting until the shelter belt has established itself.

You could also consider moving a certain amount of earth to build contoured mounds to create sheltered pockets within your site. As with all planning for shelter, the art is to balance the need for shelter against the desirability of a view out. An example is shown in the plan, below, of a house with a magnificent view down an estuary, up which comes the prevailing wind. The solution lay in a combination of planting and contouring.

Softer face of the coastal garden (right) *A glorious view of sheltered cottages and gardens across the inlet is afforded from a seaside garden where increased reflected light and shelter from frost allow a luxuriant display of "wild" planting.*

Cliff-top ruggedness (below left) *The beauty of this wind-shaped garden scene would be destroyed by any attempt at decorative gardening.*

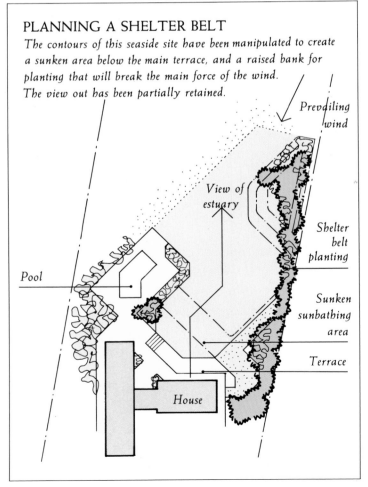

PLANNING A SHELTER BELT
The contours of this seaside site have been manipulated to create a sunken area below the main terrace, and a raised bank for planting that will break the main force of the wind. The view out has been partially retained.

Prevailing wind

View of estuary

Shelter belt planting

Sunken sunbathing area

Terrace

Pool

House

THE QUARRY GARDEN

Another form of rugged garden is inspired by the natural planting that establishes itself among the scree and larger rocks associated with old quarries or rocky upland areas. If your garden is rocky, you should regard the look as a visual bonus and adapt your gardening to suit, rather than attempting a lifetime of clearance.

There is a difference between a rocky look and a garden rockery. The rocky look is essentially a matter of ground shaping with outcrops, while the rockery should appear as solid rock with pockets of earth and general planting associated with it. Garden rockeries are expensive to make, difficult to maintain and have a limited seasonal appeal. For anyone contemplating building one, consider the idea carefully first.

The consideration of outcrops of rock as a sculptural element within the landscape is, however, intriguing, particularly when combined with plants strong enough in their own sculptural form to harmonize.

Rocky look in a valley *The rugged effect of rocks and gravel in this valley garden is enhanced by the bole of a dead tree. Ferns blend with mosses to create a slightly sinister, yet luxuriant, feel.*

The true rockery *A carpet of wild thyme (Thymus serpyllum) growing across huge lichen-covered granite rocks — mineral and vegetable forms blending miraculously together — constitutes a real rockery.*

Coarse granite scree *Forms of potentilla appreciate the hard, though well-drained, medium of coarse granite scree in a Welsh garden. Coarse scree beds are almost maintenance free.*

ROCK FORMATIONS AND PLANTS

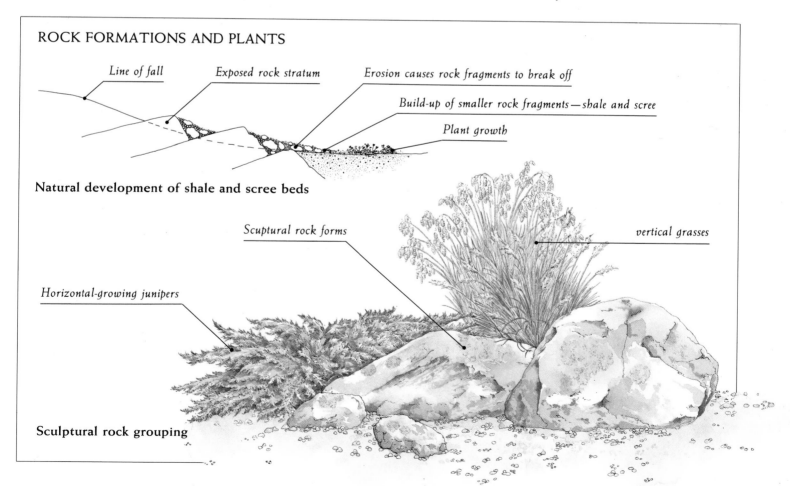

Line of fall

Exposed rock stratum

Erosion causes rock fragments to break off

Build-up of smaller rock fragments — shale and scree

Plant growth

Natural development of shale and scree beds

Sculptural rock forms

vertical grasses

Horizontal-growing junipers

Sculptural rock grouping

WOODLAND GARDEN

One of the most natural forms of garden must be that created within woodland or with a strong woodland feel. Sadly, there is very little native woodland left in Northern Europe that has not been tampered with by man. In North America there is still much native woodland although it is under threat where the land can be exploited commercially. So the study of native woodland has increased, and any remaining pockets of it should be protected at all costs. The country gardener is in the enviable position of being able to add to the woodland total, albeit in a small way, while the town gardener with a country heart will have to rely on planting lower-growing forms of tree and associated plants to create a woodland effect.

TYPES OF WOODLAND GARDEN

Your garden might be inspired by surrounding woodland, or might include within its boundaries some trees and their associated planting. It might be large enough to encompass significant groups of trees, from the smallest spinney to woodland big enough for a game covert. It may simply be dominated by one or two standard trees — the sole survivors of an ancient forest.

Whatever your garden's woodland link, you have to be clear about the type of native woodland you are living with and complementing. Each type will have its predominant type of tree, and then successive natural growth layers beneath. For the gardening element to work visually as well as practically, the plants should be selected to complement these natural layers of vegetation, for example by planting bluebells among hazel trees.

Changing fortunes (right) *A mixed grouping of mature silver birch, beech and Scots pine, which at one time was part of a northern shelter belt plantation, is now part of an enviable garden.*

Small-scale gems (left) *Late autumn cyclamen and early snowdrops make excellent winter ground-cover beneath an oakwood canopy.*

What we perceive when looking at native woodland is the climax growth of a whole profile of plants that has taken generations to develop. Just as the natural range of structural materials available for the garden varies according to the local geology, so do plant communities of which trees are the ultimate key members. Native woodland communities can be summarized as follows:

Damp oakwoods grow on deep soils, having a thickish shrub sub-layer often dominated by hazel. In open glades, ash, beech, birch, cherry and hornbeam may grow.

Dry oakwoods grow on coarse sand over sandstone. They include birch and mountain ash, which, together with the dominant oaks, create a close canopy allowing a reduced shrub layer beneath.

Beechwoods grow in chalky limestone soils or in loam over chalk and even in acid soils, as long as they are well-drained. Little grows beneath beech, although, if sparsely enough planted, whitebeam and ash may.

Ashwoods may establish themselves in damp chalky soils, often in association with hawthorn.

Pinewoods (natural as opposed to man-made forests) prefer sandy soil. Few plants will grow beneath pines, although, on their fringes, bilberry and heaths can survive.

But how does this knowledge of natural vegetation help the gardener to create a wooded country look on a small scale? It is a salutary thought that most lowland garden locations would have been forest at one time. Before the first city, town, village, hamlet, house, even the first brick, the soil was at one with its trees and their associated plants. You can introduce the spirit of woodland by planting just one or two appropriate trees and associating them with complementary lower planting.

Beech tree trunks (right) *Beech tree trunks have a monumental quality somehow emphasized by a mossy ground cover.*

Spirit of woodland (below) *One or two tree trunks in your garden will evoke the spirit of woodland, especially if you have inherited mature specimens. The two plane trees (Platanus acerifolia), left, are covered in lichen due to the dampness of a seaboard location, while the ancient, braced mulberry (Morus nigra), right—a legacy of the silk trade in England—casts its gnarled charm over a country garden in town.*

FOLIAGE

Two of the many attractive facets of the woodland garden are foliage shape and foliage colour. Foliage shape tempers the way light filters through differing densities of leaves; foliage colour comes into its own in autumn. With many trees, the intensity of leaf colour in autumn varies according to the amounts of sunlight and rainfall they receive through the preceding summer, but certain trees never fail to display. Among "wilder" species, silver birch (*Betulus* sp.), field maple (*Acer campestre*), beech (*Fagus* sp.), hornbeam (*Carpinus* sp.) and wild cherry (*Prunus avium*) colour best, with various forms of viburnum in the shrub layer beneath their canopy. But many exotic species can be associated with them, with discretion, to give a range of colour from lemon yellow through chrome, to gold, russet and deepest purple.

Two woodland walks (right and below) *Autumn in a garden full of deciduous trees is a visual delight of changing leaf colour. The bulk of mature trees, and the way their shapes interlock, creates seclusion and a sense of calm in a relatively small space.*

SPINNEYS AND COPSES

The dictionary description of a spinney is a small clump of trees, while a copse (or coppice) is a wood of small growth for periodical cutting or "coppicing". The term spinney does not evoke dense growth, but rather a sparse planting of standard trees, with open glades of younger shrubby plants beneath. New spinneys may be planted with any number of trees, although for relatively quick decorative effect, stick to forest-scale trees, and do not mix the species too heavily. Traditionally, flowering trees occurred at the edge of the mix, and those with autumn colour and/or fruit extend the spinney's interest. Species of *Malus* (the crab apples) are excellent.

The copse is a traditional form of land management in damp oakwood areas (see p. 84) where hazel (*Corylus* sp.) is planted at close intervals and periodically cut back to ground level to form a "stool". The growth removed includes many stems as thick as a broomhandle that are used to weave into hurdles. These were once used to temporarily enclose grazing sheep but now make excellent fencing material for the country garden. From a gardening point of view, developing a few hazel, dogwood or willow stools will ensure fresh, vigorous growth and strong autumn leaf colour and will create a woodland feeling even in a very small area.

PLANTING A COPSE

Where a wooded boundary is becoming too tall—with an undesirable view beneath the tree foliage canopy developing—you might consider planting a younger spinney, both as a foreground feature and as a way of increasing the effectiveness of the boundary screen.

In this case the existing planting was of birch with pine and, on the perimeter, the white-flowering Amelanchier lamarckii. *All these are re-used in a circle in front of the originals, the plan allowing for easy fencing while the trees are saplings.*

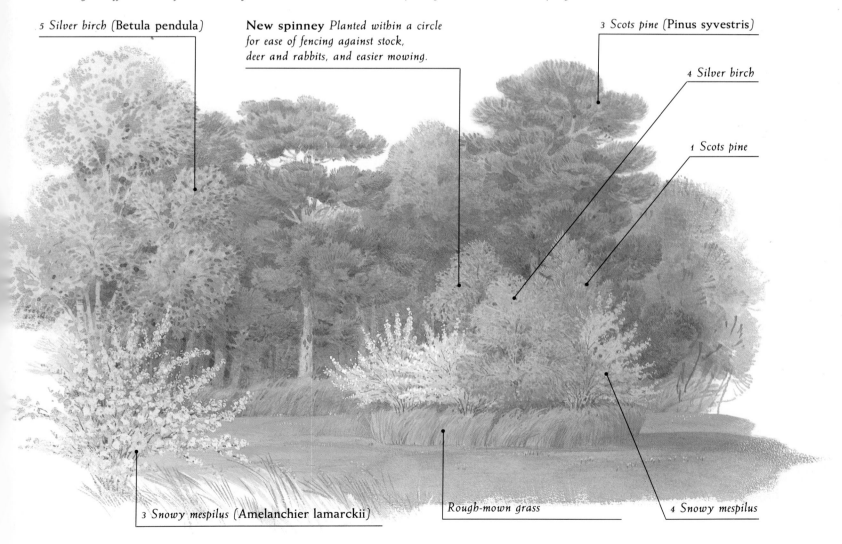

5 *Silver birch* (Betula pendula)

New spinney *Planted within a circle for ease of fencing against stock, deer and rabbits, and easier mowing.*

3 *Scots pine* (Pinus syvestris)

4 *Silver birch*

1 *Scots pine*

3 *Snowy mespilus* (Amelanchier lamarckii)

Rough-mown grass

4 *Snowy mespilus*

THE COLOUR GARDEN

For those of us living in the more northerly climes, the thought of colour outside is light at the end of a dark tunnel during the long months of winter. We pore over plant catalogues in anticipation and select a host of ill-assorted shrubs, perennials and annuals to brighten a far off summer scene. The trouble is that, while using colour as the chief criterion for the plan of your country garden is a perfectly understandable method, with many models and precedents in the history of gardening, it is a course strewn with pitfalls. The deepest of these is that the hybridization of exotic plant material (anything short of tropical), has given gardeners the possibility of a colour palette that would put a fairground in the shade. While it is possible to get away with making a riot of exotic colour in a walled town garden—for you have only yourself to blind—in the country it makes more sense to use colours that harmonize with nature's own.

COLOUR AND NATURAL GARDENING

Whilst your eye might forgive an exotic plant species in a natural garden, especially if it has a harmonious colour as well as form and texture that complement its indigenous backdrop, it is very difficult not to be offended by the violent oranges and purples of many species. Why not include the way you consider colour in your new natural country garden perspective, at least towards the boundary of your plot where the colour of the plants within your garden should harmonize with the colours outside it?

Do not forget that in many country locations, everything is seen against and within the many shades of green. And early morning,

Grey with silver birch (right) *This restful, grey foreground planting blends very well with silver birch trunks in the middle distance.*

Yellows against a cereal crop (left) *The creams and chrome yellows of foliage variegation and tobacco plant blooms blend perfectly with the harvest gold of a cereal crop in a field beyond the garden.*

sparkling dew-covered green, is quite different from the hazy blue of green in high sunlight, and soft evening light produces yet another tone. So nature's colours themselves are modified by different qualities of light, which should give you a wide tonal range from which to choose the plant material for your country garden.

Whilst the colour of the foliage of native trees is broadly green, it too varies in tone from the dark green of some native conifers and yew, which seem almost black on the skyline in winter, to the light grey-green of whitebeams (*Sorbus* sp). But there is no purple foliage that grows naturally, nor heavily variegated foliage, or that virulent glaucous blue of some introduced conifers.

FLOWER COLOUR

The colours of the flowers of the majority of native trees and shrubs are cream, lemon, white or green. Native wild flower colour also tends towards these paler colours, moving with the seasons through pinks, pale blues, then yellows and golds. Where nature establishes broad bands of one colour (and she does not often mix large masses of colour) they tend to be in light shade, such as the bluebell

HEATHER PLANTING SCHEME

The strong purples and mauve/pinks of heather deserve space. This simple scheme brings the colours of a distant moor right into a garden. The shapes of the planting areas within the garden complement nature's "moorland marquetry" (a term coined by the Scottish artist Ian Hamilton Finlay) formed by the combinations of patches of heather contrasted with patches of grassland and woodland.

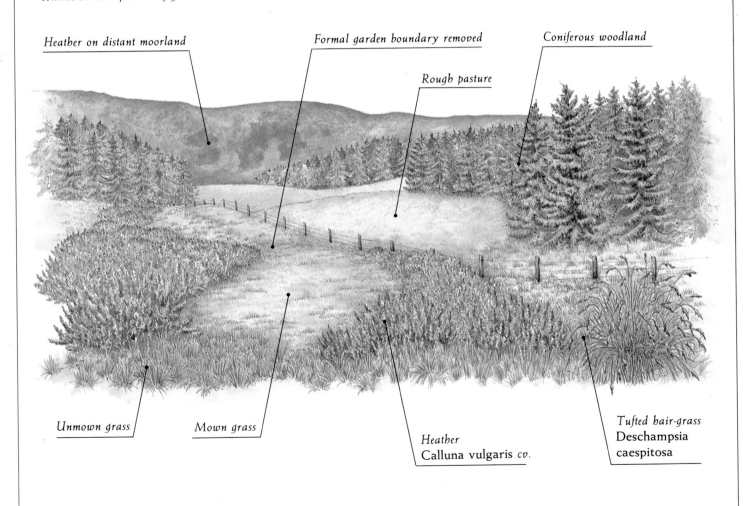

Heather on distant moorland

Formal garden boundary removed

Coniferous woodland

Rough pasture

Unmown grass

Mown grass

Heather
Calluna vulgaris *cv.*

Tufted hair-grass
Deschampsia
caespitosa

mass, or sheets of wild garlic or dog's mercury. Where there is a brilliance of natural colour, such as poppies, they usually grow amongst grass or corn, and their amazing colour is softened and diluted. It is the diluted colour effect—the mosaic of dots of colour—that is the essence of cottage garden style (see p.118).

Gertrude Jeckyll, the celebrated early twentieth-century English plantswoman, is often wrongly associated with cottage garden style. For although she admired cottage garden flowers, her use of colour was far from diluted, rather she used colour and texture as a painter might, in broad swathes. She used hotter colours in the foreground—what I now term the domestic zone A (see p.28)—and linked them to softer blues in the perimeter zone, where they blended into the cool damp light of a typical Edwardian summer's day! The use of colour in the garden is very personal, and as different people dress in particular colour ranges to suit their personality, their physical characteristics and the fashion of the day, so differing sites and locations, the period of the house, and the activities surrounding it, will dictate suitable colour ranges for your plants.

GRASSES PLANTING SCHEME

The scheme below contrasts the horticultural flower colour of perennials, planted in a single bold swathe in the foreground, with the subdued colour of naturalized grasses. The grasses are planned to complement a back-drop of open countryside, near inland water or perhaps adjacent to a seaside inlet.

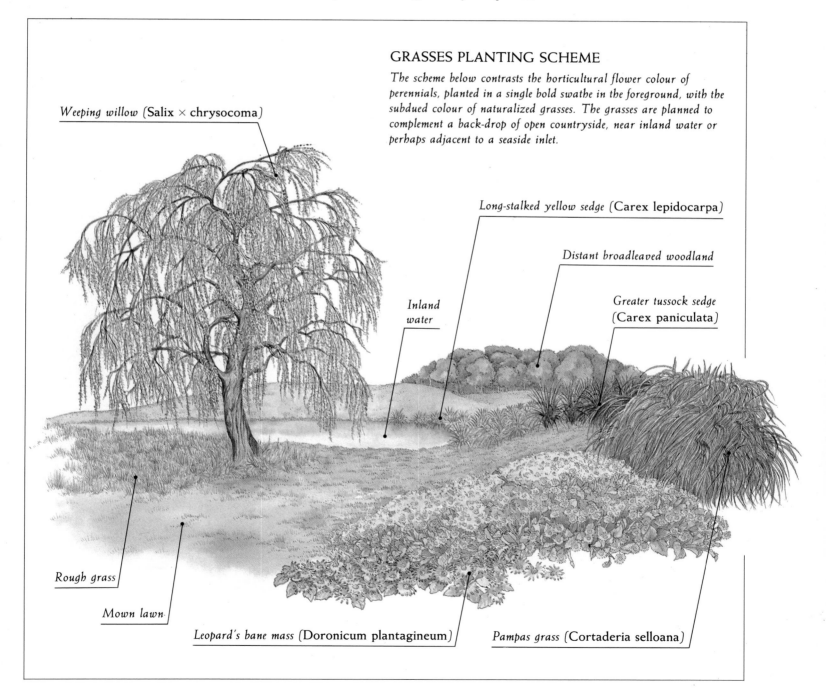

Weeping willow (Salix × chrysocoma)

Long-stalked yellow sedge (Carex lepidocarpa)

Distant broadleaved woodland

Inland water

Greater tussock sedge (Carex paniculata)

Rough grass

Mown lawn

Leopard's bane mass (Doronicum plantagineum)

Pampas grass (Cortaderia selloana)

THE GARDEN IN SPRING

When Browning reminisced, "Oh, to be in England now that April's there", it was not because the weather is particularly good—April can be terrible in Britain—but because there is a delicious expectancy in the air that accompanies the gradual reawakening. After at least two, if not three, months of feeling that winter will never end, the smallest signs of spring relieve the depression and confirm the promise of winter's brave flowers. All at once you notice that the evenings are staying lighter, and daffodils are everywhere. If you keep out of the wind, the sun is actually quite warm again. The lambs are growing fast and the earth is drying out, the birds are making a tumultuous noise in the mornings and suddenly it's fine to cut the grass again!

Another month and most trees are in leaf, even the tulips are here. A haunting cuckoo call carries across the fields and, in the woods, bluebells push through the groundcover of dog's mercury. It's an enchanted time, when you need to be outside. Little wonder that the pagans danced to celebrate the spring equinox, to convey that winter was finally felt to be dead and buried.

NATURE'S PATTERNS

As wild flowers begin to show in spring, take special note of nature's planting patterns before lusher growth makes them more difficult to discern. Observe the random scatter of primroses along a bank, for example, or the drifts of wild bulbs that have spread over many years. These are the patterns you will want to interpret in your garden as you sow and plant for the year ahead, and for next spring: strengthening an effect here, possibly, and removing a mistake there.

The bluebell wood
(right) *An English bluebell (Scilla non-scripta) wood in May is a classic model for the natural gardener. Sheets of blue carpet the ground beneath beech trees (Fagus sylvatica).*

Wild primroses (left)
The wild primrose (Primula vulgaris), appears on damp mossy banks in early spring. Its purity of colour is matched only by its sharp, spicy fragrance.

SPRING FLOWER COLOUR

Flowers from bulbs provide the predominant colours in the cultivated spring garden, but in the natural country garden they should simply complement native species, just as the narcissus combine with dandelions (*Taraxacum officinale*) and pale blue speedwell (*Veronica officinalis*) in the photograph opposite.

Unfortunately, hybridization has led to the development of showy plant forms that bear little resemblance to their natural parents. The natural colours of the spring garden are quite subtle—the new greens of tree and grass foliage, for example—and it is all too easy to allow strident cultivated colours to ruin them. Strong pink, for instance, is not a spring colour in the wild, where lemon and yellow predominate. Strong blues are usually diffused in a mass of greenery. Save strong-coloured bulbs for planting in the proximity of the house and terrace.

Sugar pink tulips *Such a strong colour combination of pink tulips with forget-me-nots is stunning in isolation against a building.*

Narcissus *Choose the smaller species for naturalizing. They are more resistant to wind and look perfect in the natual garden.*

Lily-flowered tulips *Lily-flowered tulips (Kaufmanniana hybrids) provide a delicate compromise between man-made and wild forms.*

Broom *Cultivated brooms provide a warm splash of delicate spring colour. This is the form Cytisus scoparius 'Sulphureus'.*

Bugle and bluebells *Bugle with bluebells makes a striking semi-wild spring plant combination for a shaded corner.*

Parrot tulips *Flopping, naturalized parrot tulips (Greigii hybrids) make a striking feature growing in an old stone wall.*

SPRING BULBS

The earliest spring flowers are those of the bulbs, and
whether they were newly-planted last autumn, or are old friends re-appearing
in time-honoured fashion, they are equally welcome. This selection of
narcissus, with anemones and some of the blue-flowering bulbs,
has enough natural charm for any country look.

Narcissus *'Golden Ducat'* (left)
A mid-season double (in bud)

Narcissus *'Blaris'*
A modern daffodil hybrid

Narcissus minor *Perhaps a
form of N.pseudonarcissus,
but to 15 cm (6 in)*

Narcissus *'Telemonius
Plenus' A double form
established in Italy
in the 17th century*

Narcissus
*'Ice follies' Early
spring to mid-spring,
large-cupped narcissus*

**Narcissus
pseudonarcissus**
(above) *This is the
commom daffodil
of early spring*

**Narcissus
pseudonarcissus
subsp. moschatus**
*A pale form native
to the Pyrennees*

Narcissus pseudonarcissus
(above) *Wild form*

Narcissus *'Hawera'*
A delicate hybrid between
N. triandus and
N. jonquilla

Narcissus *'Cragford'*
Horticultural form of the
Tazetta narcissus group

Narcissus *'Langwith'*
A trumpet narcissus

Narcissus *'Penvose'*
Modern daffodil hybrid

Narcissus tazetta *cv.*
Fragrant horticultural form

Grape-hyacinth
(Muscari
armeniacum)
Likes full sun and
well-drained soil

Scilla sibirica
A native of woods,
scrub and screes

Anemone blanda
'White splendour'
Flowers as much as
5 cm (2 in) across

Anemone blanda (below)
Best under deciduous
trees in light shade

Glory-of-the-snow
(Chionodoxa luciliae)
Grows naturally on
stony hillsides

PLANTING FOR SPRING

Most gardeners are conditioned to planting a comparatively limited range of spring bulbs when there is a much wider range available, especially for the country garden. Take the genus *Allium* for instance, species of which start flowering in late spring. They are easy to grow in any light, well-drained soil and prefer a sunny position. Many,

Mixed spring collection (left) *The dappled shade cast by small trees provides ideal conditions for dog's tooth violet (*Erythronium dens-canis*) amongst* Arum pictum *and a sheet of* Muscari *sp.*

particularly the smaller forms, (*A. moly* and *A. azureum* for example) increase themselves rapidly and are therefore excellent plants to establish in gravel (see p. 104).

Anemones are excellent for the semi-wild look. *Anemone apennia* and *A. blanda* (see p. 97) both do well in sun or light shade, and increase and ramble in light woodland. The true woodland anemone is *A. nemerosa* and it prefers a damp situation.

Chionodoxa sp. Glory of the Snow, has charming clear blue flowers—so named because they bloom as the snow

PLANTING SCHEME FOR A GRAVEL OASIS WITH SPRING-FLOWERING BULBS

A birch grove can make a wonderful transition from garden to countryside, and is the ideal location for various naturalized, *spring-flowered bulbs. Here is a planting scheme for bulb masses between silver birches on either side of a gravel path.*

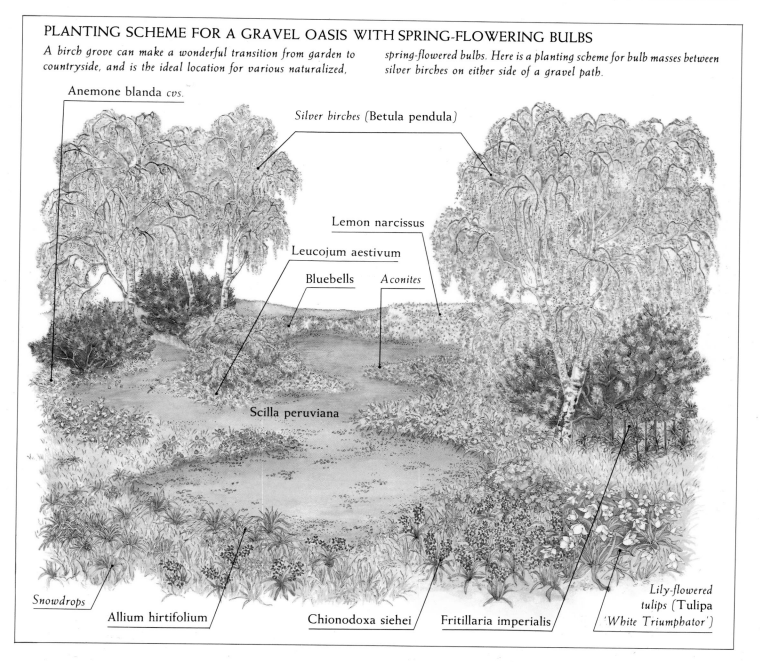

Anemone blanda *cvs.*

Silver birches (Betula pendula)

Lemon narcissus

Leucojum aestivum

Bluebells   *Aconites*

Scilla peruviana

Snowdrops

Allium hirtifolium

Chionodoxa siehei

Fritillaria imperialis

Lily-flowered tulips (Tulipa 'White Triumphator')

melts in the mountains of Turkey. It likes the sun and good drainage and is therefore an ideal gravel bulb. Plant them in association with the similarly blue-flowered *Scilla spp,* which will spread themselves rapidly.

Species of the dog's tooth violet genus, *Erythronium,* are real eye-stoppers in damp semi-shade. Their foliage, as well as their unusual flowers are excellent.

The fritillaries, with their bell-like flowers, are plants around which fairy stories could be written. There are visual goodies and baddies amongst them. The goodies are the delicate little snake's head fritillaries (*Fritillaria meleagris*), which have unparalleled charm when established in grass and do best in semi-shaded conditions. The baddies are the crown imperials, *F. imperials,* which have great stately heads of hanging flowers (either yellow or orange red) and prefer sun and loam.

TULIPS

Species tulip, of which there are many forms, flower earlier than the ubiquitous forms of bedding tulip in the main and are much smaller. Many (*Tulipa clusiana* and *T. tarda,* for example) have flowers which open fully like lilies in sun. The Greigii hybrids also have beautiful striped foliage. To naturalize tulips, you have to plant bulbs at least 15cm (6 in) deep in a well-drained soil, preferably in sun. Over a period of years, the size of naturalized plants and their flowers decrease, but this process often increases their natural charm.

AFTER THE BULBS

As the bulb flowers begin to die, springtime moves on to scenes of lambs under orchard blossom—the very soft pink blossom of apple and pear. Natural tree blossoms, including cherry (*Prunus avium*), the bird cherry (*Prunus padus*), wild crab apple (*Malus sylvestris*) and blackthorn (*Prunus spinosa*), are all white sometimes turning to cream. As with bulb flowers, sugar pink and red blossoms have an alien look and have to be used very carefully in the overall scene especially if backed by landscape. It is best to avoid them or to use them against darker coniferous greens for maximum effect.

Tulips for border planting (right) *Tulips can be a very successful ingredient in a mixed border scheme. This pink and yellow combination is backed by irises, hostas and bergenias.*

Cherry blossom (below) *The particularly fine cherry,* Prunus 'Ukon', *framing a view across the lawn in my garden, has pale yellow semi-double flowers that blend with the fresh green foliage of spring.*

SPRING BLOSSOM

The joy of seeing the first blossom unfurling from bursting buds is undiminished no matter how many times you have seen it before. It affirms the health of the garden as it stirs itself from winter's sleep, and its transient beauty and fragrance is a promise of fruits to come.

Common pear (Pyrus communis) *Cultivated pears are indistinguishable from wild ones*

Lilac (Syringa × diversifolia) *A hybrid whose panicles of white flowers are particularly early*

Blackthorn or sloe (Prunus spinosa) *Small white flowers usually precede the leaves*

Siberian crab (Malus baccata), left. *The delicate white blossom of a naturalized species of crab apple*

Bird cherry (Prunus padus) *Fragrant flowers are born in spreading racemes*

Cherry laurel (Prunus laurocerasus) *Racemes of tiny, creamy white flowers seen against shiny green leaves*

Cultivated cherry (Prunus '*Ukon*'), right. *Semi-double flowers tinted yellowish-green*

Cultivated cherry (Prunus '*Shirofugen*'), above. *Double flowers, the palest of pinks in bud, white on opening*

Snowdrop tree (Halesia carolina) *A beautiful north American native with creamy, bell-shaped flowers*

Plum (Prunus domestica '*Plantierensis*') *The creamy white blossom of this double-flowered form of plum*

Gean cherry (Prunus avium '*Plena*') *Profusely flowering, snowy white form*

THE GRAVEL GARDEN

Gravel is being used increasingly as a ground-covering medium having a number of advantages. Texturally, it is an intermediate between the hard pavings — brick, stone and concrete — and the softness of grass. Design-wise it works as a transition between the two, making both an all-weather, practical surfacing and, with plants, a decorative space as well. An area of gravel can be seen as another element within the collage of your overall garden design too (see p.40), linking visually with, say, the house structure and outbuildings, or perhaps just the garden wall that it adjoins.

The proliferation of sit-on mowers which need wide turning circles and cannot negotiate tight corners, has created many an awkward country garden corner, ideal for gravel surfacing.

CONSOLIDATED CONSTRUCTION TECHNIQUE

The gravel surfacing that I advocate is not the sort of soft and crunchy morass that clings like a bog (although as a burglar deterrent in certain situations this is not a bad idea); it is hard and consolidated, similar to a French market place on which the locals play *boules*. If necessary, the surface should be retained by a curb such as brick-on-edge.

To create such an area, excavate to approximately 75mm (3 in) depending on your soil — more for clay and sand, less for flint or stones. Roll and consolidate into this 60mm (2½ in) of unwashed gravel or ballast. This will have clay amongst it and it will bind together with moisture to become hard. Into this roll and consolidate the top layer of finished, preferably rounded, pea shingle — the type of gravel that has been dug from pits and smoothed by the action of water. This medium

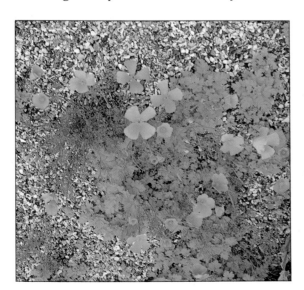

Gravel as a foil (right)
Not only is well-consolidated gravel a first-rate surface to walk on, it also serves as a fine visual foil to plants with strong form.

Self-seeders (left)
*Annual orange Californian poppies (*Eschscholtzia *sp.) self-seed in gravel and combine well with golden feverfew (*Chrysanthemum parthenium*).*

is kinder to small children if they fall over in it. However, in areas where there is a naturally occurring stone, you will find the local gravel is a quarried version of it. Although the medium will be sharper-edged, it will be a perfect visual match to your local materials.

The finished, rolled surface will be semi-porous and over a period, dust will collect in it and weeds will inevitably self-seed. But if these will regenerate and flourish, so will masses of garden plants and it is the random, woolly effect which this surfacing encourages that is so attractive.

Maintenance could not be more simple. When the weedy look gets too much for you, simply hoe through the top surface of gravel on a hot, sunny day so that unwanted growth is cut away or uprooted, then dries and dies. The odd out-of-place seedling can be weeded out by hand most easily after rain. Light raking and the occasional top dressing with fresh gravel will revive "tired" areas.

Gravelled corner *The thistle,* Eryngium giganteum *'Miss Wilmotts's Ghost', is a great self-seeder. Here it is growing in gravel together with hollyhocks.*

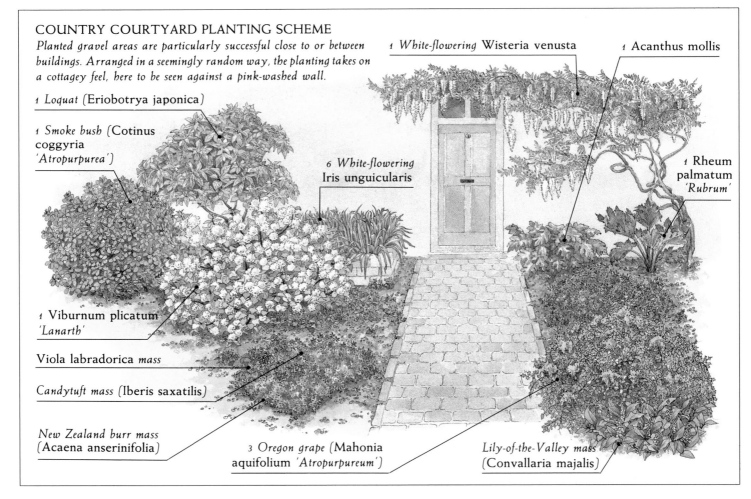

COUNTRY COURTYARD PLANTING SCHEME
Planted gravel areas are particularly successful close to or between buildings. Arranged in a seemingly random way, the planting takes on a cottagey feel, here to be seen against a pink-washed wall.

1 Loquat (Eriobotrya japonica)

1 Smoke bush (Cotinus coggyria *'Atropurpurea'*)

1 White-flowering Wisteria venusta

1 Acanthus mollis

6 White-flowering Iris unguicularis

1 Rheum palmatum *'Rubrum'*

1 Viburnum plicatum *'Lanarth'*

Viola labradorica *mass*

Candytuft mass (Iberis saxatilis)

New Zealand burr mass (Acaena anserinifolia)

3 Oregon grape (Mahonia aquifolium *'Atropurpureum'*)

Lily-of-the-Valley mass (Convallaria majalis)

PLANTING IN GRAVEL

As well as waiting for the natural self-seeding of plants in the dust build-up in gravel surfacing, you can create planting pockets within the medium and so establish the natural look very quickly.

Take a crowbar and pierce the newly-laid gravel and its consolidated base, to make a hole that you can enlarge with a spade. Backfill this hole with fertile soil, planting your subject as you do so. Include the odd woody plant that will enjoy the well-drained conditions, perhaps shrub roses or cistus. Many herbs and grey-foliaged plants will also thrive happily in gravel.

Where the gravel is prevented from spilling into planting areas by a curb, plants will naturally spread out and disguise the edging. However, the edging can be further blurred by planting at random through the gravel on the "wrong" side of the curb.

Nasturtiums *The dwarf annual varieties of the genus* Tropaeolum, *will pop up through a dry gravel medium, and then self-seed.*

Pansies *The tiny herbaceous perennials of the genus* Viola, *are excellent for planting out and "naturalizing" in gravel.*

Lysimachia nummularia 'Aurea' *Creeping Jenny is a delightful specimen for gravel. This example has bright gold foliage.*

Taxus repens 'Aurea' *The low-growing, golden variegated yew makes a good evergreen skeleton shrub through gravel.*

Verbascum olympicum *Felty rosettes represent the yearling plants of this biennial, which will develop a yellow flower spike.*

Ajuga reptans 'Atropurpurea' *Makes a good groundcover in partial shade, having blue flower spikes in early summer.*

THE FLOWER GARDEN

Having considered the use of colour in the country garden (the rules for which apply just as much to foliage as to flowers), let us look at the various forms of flower-only gardening and see how they fit into the country garden today. For many gardeners the quantity of flowers in any garden is still the criterion by which the excellence of that garden is judged; but they are missing so much else. The numerous horticultural publications, public authorities and plant merchants' catalogues encourage people to regard blast upon blast of randomly mixed, garish flower colours as the gardener's only goal.

Such an attitide belittles the natural beauty of flowers, which, in their native or less hybridized forms have a balance of shape, structure, colour and often a fragrance, that combine to provide one of life's great delights. The unthinking use of ever bigger and brighter blooms only detracts from each individual specimen's attributes and overshadows the gentler charms of native flowers.

SYMPATHETIC USE OF FLOWER COLOUR

The natural country garden calls for a use of flower colour that reserves brighter displays for schemes to be seen in association with buildings. Elsewhere in the garden it must complement local indigenous planting, especially where flowers will be seen against the country backdrop. Using wild flowers exclusively is a form of gardening that is gaining great popularity (see p.116).

Where a bright, mixed flower garden is inappropriate, and you want to grow flowers for cutting, you might consider using them in rows or blocks as in a vegetable garden, where they can look spectacular.

Massed flowers used successfully (right) *Massed flowers can be spectacularly successful when used in a definite colour scheme, especially when seen against buildings, such as this French farmhouse.*

Flowers in the kitchen garden (left) *Surely no more pleasant job exists than cutting flowers on a summer morning? Here larkspur and delphiniums are being cut for drying from massed ranks in the kitchen garden.*

ROSES

No climate allows a longer flowering period for roses than does that of the United Kingdom, where many roses will bloom all summer—and that is unique. Most other places in the world have late spring and early summer roses—but the flowers do not last further into the year. So it is not surprising that the rose is very much part of the English summer flower garden scene.

The rose garden *per se* is now something of a period concept, for it assumes that outside the rose blooming season there are other parts of the garden to which one can go. Nowadays, it is more pertinent to recognize that there are types of rose that combine excellently with other plants in the mixed border.

OLD-FASHIONED FORMS FOR NEW GARDENS
For myself, the type of rose that best fits into the more natural garden is undoubtedly the shrub rose, a large category that encompasses various types including wild roses, traditional old garden roses and modern shrub roses—a

grouping of roses that I collectively term old-fashioned. The newer shrub roses have an extended flowering period, which the older ones did not, though their "improved" flower forms may come at the expense of their fragrance.

Most important, however, is that shrub roses in the main grow into a bush shape that has character, with the added advantage of coloured hips in the autumn. Shrub roses can look well simply as specimen shrubs amongst rough grass, or used as part of a hedge, for many have a natural grace, both in and out of flower. The attributes of the plant extend to climbing and rambling forms that will complement old walls or ramble into fruit trees.

Against a shady backdrop (right) *The colour of this briar hybrid shrub rose 'Cerise Bouquet' is strengthened when contrasted with a dark, shady backdrop. Its form is open, relaxed and graceful.*

A rose for cutting (below) *This beautiful, pink in bud, white in flower, hybrid tea rose, 'Tamora', has dark glossy foliage and makes an excellent flower for cutting and arranging.*

FLOWERS FOR CUTTING

It is strange that while one's house might be surrounded with flowers in summer, big bunches of flowers, like that opposite (including white shasta daisies, *Echinops ritro* and lavender) are still irresistible for cutting and bringing indoors to put into vases.

Most of us have favourite flowers for cutting. They will have been selected through personal reminiscences, romantic associations, the style of your house interior and, more practically, what lasts longest in water. It is best to cut flowers in the morning when the dew has gone, but before the sun is hot. This way the stem contains the maximum amount of moisture, and the flowers will be at their best, fully open and not yet drooping. Prior to arranging the flowers in a suitable container, it is a good idea to stand them for a while in deep cool water in the shade, as in the example opposite.

Teasels *One of the loveliest of wild flowers (or fruiting heads) for cutting is Fullers' teasel (Dipsacus fullonum).*

Sidalcea *The tall spires of pink sidalcea, a hardy perennial of the mallow family, make a dramatic contribution to any arrangement.*

Salvia *Hardy herbaceous perennial forms of salvia are an ever reliable source of cut flowers with country charm.*

Chrysanthemums and asters *Shasta daisies and mauve-blue* Aster frikartii, *are both excellent for cutting.*

Delphinium cultivars *The huge pink flowerheads of double annual larkspur (Delphinium sp.) are excellent cut fresh.*

Looking for the unusual *Be on the look out for unlikely flowerheads to spice your displays, such as these heads of echinops.*

WILDFLOWER GARDENING

The romantic associations of wild flowers, their reported demise through the spraying programmes demanded by modern forms of agriculture, and the possibility of turning some spare piece of land into something pretty, have combined all of a sudden to popularize the concept of wild-flower gardening. Add to this the ecological favours of protecting the homes of endangered species of bug, and providing food for your local fauna, and the idea cannot fail to appeal to country gardeners.

However, the reality is something else. If you cultivate a piece of ground by rotovator and leave it, the most invasive indigenous or naturalized plant species that you always thought were weeds will colonize it and flower.

If you fail to cut the lawn for a week or two (as we are all aware after a holiday) you will have a wildflower lawn that will look very well when contrasted with mown lawn. With the addition of naturalized spring bulbs this is probably the

most practical sort of wildflower garden that most of us should aspire to for a relatively quick result.

CREATING A WILDFLOWER MEADOW

The wildflower purist who wants a virgin wildflower meadow should consider the work involved. Native grasses in the main grow too vigorously to allow seedling wild flowers to establish themselves, so sprinkling packets of wild flowers in the lawn is not the way. What is required first is the destruction of the existing coarse perennial grasses and any other tenacious plant. It is a paradox that to do this you may have to use the very weedkiller which has destroyed the wild flowers we long to see!

Across this virgin territory you sow a *prepared wildflower and fine grass seed mix*. It is essential that this is suitable for your particular soil both for its own well being, and along with the consideration that it would be an act of vandalism

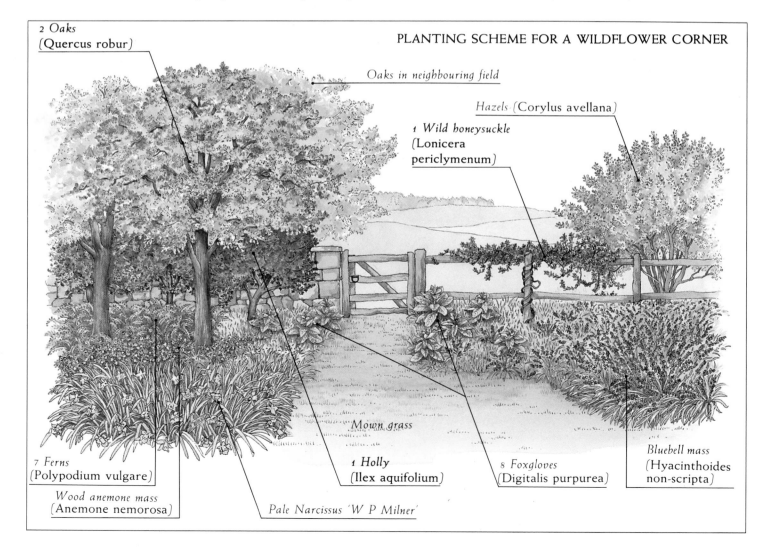

PLANTING SCHEME FOR A WILDFLOWER CORNER

2 Oaks
(Quercus robur)

Oaks in neighbouring field

Hazels (Corylus avellana)

1 Wild honeysuckle
(Lonicera periclymenum)

7 Ferns
(Polypodium vulgare)

Wood anemone mass
(Anemone nemorosa)

Mown grass

Pale Narcissus 'W P Milner'

1 Holly
(Ilex aquifolium)

8 Foxgloves
(Digitalis purpurea)

Bluebell mass
(Hyacinthoides non-scripta)

to introduce alien wild species on any scale into a landscape environment with which it is not in accord. This sort of wildflower meadow may take up to three years to establish itself as the Monet'esque tapestry that you hold in your mind's eye.

A painfully tedious alternative to this method of establishing the wildflower meadow, is to buy seedling wild species from a specialist nursery (or raise them yourself), which you grow on and plant out amongst established meadow grass. With maintenance these more mature specimens will be able to compete with the vigour of natives already growing there.

Grazed meadow look (right) *This kind of traditional grazed meadow look can be achieved by sowing mixed grasses with red clover* (Trifolium pratense), *daisies* (Bellis perennis) *and buttercups* (Ranunculus bulbosus) *mixed in with them.*

Flowery boundary (below) *In the lush, flowery period of late spring, encroaching wild flowers and grasses such as ragged Robin (here seen against foaming umbels of Queen Anne's Lace) can make a dramatic backdrop.*

FLOWERS FOR DRYING

There is an increasing interest in growing flowers that can be dried and used in arrangements for decoration. Many perennial flowers are suitable, some of which may be part of the country garden anyway. In this category are *Alchemilla mollis*, achillea, sedum heads, many of the thistles, and nearly all the grasses. Annuals may be grown, specially for drying (including grasses, *Helipterum* sp., cornflowers and marigolds) in broad swathes, amongst perennial masses in borders, or in the kitchen garden.

For the country dweller, the fields and hedgerows are a further source of plant material for drying—not just flowers, seedheads, cones, ferns and mosses, but also the stems of climbers such as wild clematis for twisting into wreaths, and twigs and branches for base material.

DRYING METHODS

There are a number of ways to dry plant material. The easiest, air drying, is simply a matter of hanging the flowers in small bunches with the heads down, in shaded, dry, airy conditions for a week or two, having first removed any leaves from the stems where they will touch in the binding. Or, if the stems are rigid enough, the flowers can be left to stand dry, in buckets or old bottles, arranged to allow air circulation between the stems and around the flower heads. Flowers such as delphiniums dry better after standing initially in a little water that you allow to disappear.

Plants with textured leaves, that do not lend themselves to any of the other methods of drying, are traditionally preserved with a mixture of one part glycerine to two parts of hot water. The plant material becomes saturated with the glycerine, turning flowers and leaves a beige tone. Stems should be left to stand in the mixture, and large individual leaves should be immersed in it.

Poppy seedheads (right) *Poppy heads can be dried, attached to florist's wire and included in decorative arrangements, where they may be combined with acorns, nuts and pine cones.*

Hang drying (below) *In the summer, you can hang dry flowers (such as this lavender) outside, in an airy but shady spot.*

THE COTTAGE GARDEN

The popular image of the typical cottage gardener is of a gentle, white-haired old lady, bumbling through flowers, with a friendly cat rolling amongst carpets of pinks at her feet. Herbs hang from kitchen beams or in the parlour ready to distil into homely remedies.

In fact, the dear old lady moved out ages ago. The new owners probably only weekend there with their two children and a retriever. These are the new country cottagers and where the old lady had an orchard which her husband scythed, Jacob's sheep now run free and their wool is woven at winter evening classes.

CHANGES OF USE

The cottage garden was once a place where a random mass of showy flowers and a vegetable patch represented brief respite from hard agricultural toil. Now its owners see the countryside that surrounds their cottage as charming and a place for relaxation, even if it is wholly agricultural. They are ecologically-minded, keen to preserve the character of their cottage and want a garden that suits their style.

They find, however, that what the local garden centre peddles is not for them. Its merchandise is too urban and they want planting that complements the countryside around them as well as the building they have refurbished with care. The only requirement shared by traditional and new cottagers is that the garden look should still thrive on neglect so that precious hours spent at the cottage are not consumed in endless garden chores. It is also the low maintenance aspect that might encourage the country gardener in town to reproduce the new cottage style, although here the look will be contained.

The dream garden
(right) *Sun-kissed poppies against a backdrop of floribunda roses, with a white rambler tumbling through the hedgerow: the cottage gardener's idyll.*

Geraniums at the cottage window (left) *The classic cottage window-sill plants, geraniums (Pelargonium sp.), are ideal for the weekender, since they require little care.*

New cottage garden style still has much to do with the use of colour. Sticking to a well defined plant colour scheme is a sure way to make strong visual links both between the garden and the cottage, and the garden and the countryside beyond. Weatherboard (or clapboard) clad cottages will have a stain or paint colour to complement. Clay-built or rendered elevations are traditionally colour-washed. Brick and stone-built cottages have a wide but subtle range of wall tones to consider and, as with all cottages, have painted window frames and doorways, the colours of which must inspire your choice of plant colour.

When thinking about harmony with colours outside your cottage garden, remember the changes of colour with season, particularly how the colour of maturing cereal crops can dominate countryside landscapes at a time when many country garden style plants are at their peak.

INCLUDING A SURPRISE ELEMENT
An unexpected element has always been part of the essence of country garden style. The surprise element can be a sculptural incident (perhaps a piece of topiary if not true sculpture) that combines well with surrounding plant forms, or it might be the inclusion of vegetables and/or fruit amongst the predominantly decorative planting. What about including artichokes and the fennels, some asparagus perhaps, then in winter there are coloured kales and the striking stems of kohl-rabi.

Herbs are very much part of the cottage garden scene under all sorts of guises and in multifarious leaf colours and shapes, since they are such good all-round garden plants. By these I mean rosemary, for instance, and lavender, and all the sages and thymes. Parsley makes a charming cottage garden edging plant.

GARDENING WITHOUT OBLIGATIONS
All these plants will add decorative as well as culinary value to the new cottage garden. And—since so many cottage owners are urban during the week—there is an added bonus and pleasure in being able to take vegetables and flowers back to town, without the obligation of a full scale vegetable garden.

For many the whole point of a cottage-type garden is its lack of obligation. The high-maintenance precedent set by picture book gardens and those "open to the public", is inhibiting rather than encouraging to those who have neither the time nor the inclination to maintain their garden to these standards.

The cottage garden gate (right) *Golden marjoram, sage and mints make up much of the planting that frames the classic picket gate to this traditional cottage garden.*

Cornish cottage garden (below left) *A profusion of herbs and grasses surrounds this Cornish cottage, linking it to the fields beyond its random hedge. The garden is alive with bees and butterflies.*

Fusing culinary interest with cottage tradition (below right) *This view shows part of the well-known vegetable garden at Barnsley House in Gloucestershire. Glorious vegetables in the foreground are mixed with lavender and standard rose bushes beyond.*

PLANNING A COTTAGE SCHEME

Once the builders move out, and the garden is secure from the incursions of surrounding livestock, the new cottage garden can start to take shape.

Begin by considering the colour ranges that exist in your landscape through the seasons. Rugged hills and moorlands will give a background of muted browns, greens and mauves, while a predominantly agricultural countryside can produce a landscape of fresh greens and bright yellows in midsummer. Consider also the materials of your home, the colour of the stone, slate and wood—particularly their colour. Then start to select your plants, all the time imagining how they will look in maturity, once established against your cottage. Think of foliage as well as flower colour, the plant's height after a fixed timescale of, say, five years, and the shape and general proportion of the plant.

PLANTING SCHEME FOR NEUTRAL WALLS

The cottage planting scheme, below, is planned to be seen against the traditional elevations of a south-of-England cottage, which has a weatherboarded upper storey over buff-coloured walls below. It would work well against any similarly neutral walls.

There is a strong skeleton of evergreen plants, including yews, viburnums, Choisya ternata and the spectacular golden-leaved Lonicera nitida 'Baggesen's Gold'. This year-round plant material is a strong support for the more traditional perennial and annual cottage-style plants.

1 Whitebeam (Sorbus aria 'Lutescens')

3 Lonicera nitida 'Baggesen's Gold'

1 Philadelphus lemoinei 'Erectus'

1 Clematis montana 'Alba'

2 Fastigiate yews (Taxus bacatta 'Fastigiata')

6 Foxgloves (Digitalis grandiflora)

1 Lonicera halliana

1 Fasatigiate yew

Shrub rose

7 Santolina incana

Marigold mass (Calendula officinalis)

1 Mexican orange (Choisya ternata)

5 Lamb's ears (Stachys lanata)

4 Anemone japonica alba

4 Stinking hellebores (Helleborus foetidus)

6 Rudbeckia deamii

3 Viburnum tinus

The two schemes below illustrate two different cottage planting schemes, each inspired by a specific cottage type. And since cottage types depend on local building traditions and materials, then the garden is guaranteed to complement the location too.

The scheme, below left, was designed for a traditional farm cottage in Sussex, in the south of England. It is constructed in brick with dark-stained weather boarding (or clapboard) across the first floor. The type has many permutations in the United Kingdom and United States. The planting creates the expected soft tumble of shrubby and perennial plantings in a colour scheme of brick-yellow with lemon and grey.

The scheme, below right, is styled for a north of England farmhouse with a fine stone barn adjacent to it. The house is a shade of green with old gold coloured window surrounds, a combination that inspires the colour scheme for the planting of pink and mauve with a creamy gold. The planting is designed to be seen both against the house and the beautiful Lakeland countryside that exists beyond this view, although it would also work, to an extent, in isolation in an enclosed garden.

SEMI-WILD SCHEME FOR COLOURED WALLS

This planting plan has a strong colour scheme of mauves and purples with yellow and white, planned to be seen against aquamarine colour-washed walls — a traditional pigment. The scheme has a semi-natural feel since it includes native plants such as holly, ivy and gorse. The visual forms of giant hogweed and gorse are also strong enough to complement an adjoining stone barn.

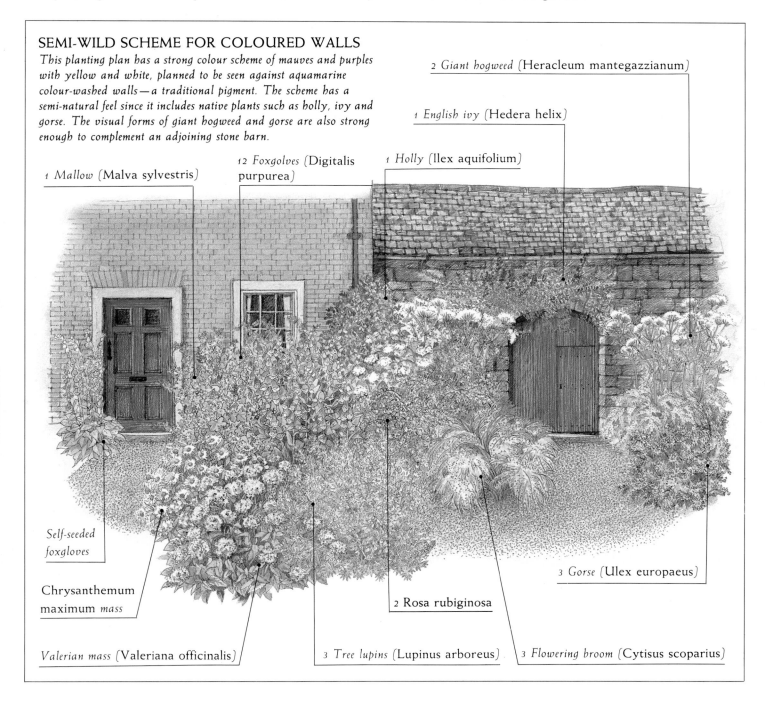

2 *Giant hogweed* (Heracleum mantegazzianum)

1 *English ivy* (Hedera helix)

1 *Holly* (Ilex aquifolium)

1 *Mallow* (Malva sylvestris)

12 *Foxgolves* (Digitalis purpurea)

Self-seeded foxgloves

Chrysanthemum maximum *mass*

Valerian mass (Valeriana officinalis)

3 *Tree lupins* (Lupinus arboreus)

2 Rosa rubiginosa

3 *Flowering broom* (Cytisus scoparius)

3 *Gorse* (Ulex europaeus)

COTTAGE GARDEN PLANTS

Given the correct soil and aspect you can, of course, grow any plant in a cottage garden; but it is not any plant that will produce the effect shown opposite, with its relaxed charm, including the noble flower spikes of the Welsh onion (*Allium fistulosum*). Few of the latest hybrids with their gross double blooms and hectic colours suit. Softer perennial plant forms and flower colours should prevail over the bolder, architectural range of plants. Climbers have an important role, and there should be a range of winter flowers, along with masses of bulbs throughout the year. Lilies are a necessary ingredient, particularly the beautiful *Lilium candidum*, which always seems to be grown in rows in traditional cottage gardens. And roses too, in their climbing, rambling and shrub forms—standards, bush and hybrid teas are too sophisticated. Herbs, with some vegetables and fruit, make up the cottage garden palette.

Decorative value of vegetables *Like many food plants, the runner bean is highly decorative in its own right.*

Shrub roses *A cottage garden would not be complete without shrub roses, in this case* Rosa canina 'Andersonii'—*a form of the dog briar.*

Massed perennials *Swathes of perennial veronica, ruby red asters and blue* Campanula lactiflora, *make the classic cottage look.*

Perennial daisy flowers *The epitome of the cottage garden flower for full sun is the single form of* Chrysanthemum maximum.

Bulbs Allium giganteum *(marvellous for dried flower arrangements) represents the bulbs that contribute to the cottage garden.*

Honesty Honesty (Lunaria annua) *is a hardy garden biennial for light shade, shown here with* Omphalodes cappadocica.

ENCHANTED GARDEN

We have seen how, looking away from the house towards the boundary, the successful country garden welds itself into the surrounding countryside, while looking back to the house, the garden is styled to suit the building. But in the intervening zone (see p.28) it is possible to create yet another style that has to relate to neither, and this we might call the enchanted garden. It is often the part of a garden that fixes itself most strongly in the memory.

You do not necessarily need a large area to bring this idea to fruition, for while on the one hand it *could* be a walled garden, on the other the feeling of the enchanted garden can be evoked by a small visual incident that transports the imagination, sitting like a punctuation mark in the overall rhythm of the layout. Planting on its own is too transitory to fill the bill, while a seat, although useful for the enjoyment of the "other-ness" of the enchanted garden, is too mundane. Some sculptural form is needed, what in the eighteenth century was termed an "eyecatcher".

COUNTRY GARDEN ORNAMENT

Most garden ornament is too grand by half, and it immediately looks pretentious placed in a modest layout. Classic sculpture is for classic layouts unless of course you use it with humour. Far better is a humbler feature—some beautifully constructed beehives perhaps, or a trophy of garden implements, or a simple piece of sculpture, not abstract, but a piece that makes a clear outline in concrete, stone or terracotta. Associated with the correct plant grouping, or contrasted with wildness, this combination contains more charm on the scale of the average garden than a dozen temples or urns.

Magic in the garden (right) *The happy abandonment of this faun gambolling in swathes of ramsons and wild parsley is very believable.*

Enchanting detail (left) *This frog spouting water forms part of a sculpture by Simon Verity, in the garden at Barnsley House, in the west of England.*

SCULPTURAL ORNAMENTS

The torso carved from fossilized rock (by Simon Verity) set amongst planting, opposite, represents a use of sculpture far removed from the placement of classical pieces in the garden. Once used to culminate a view moulded by hedging or trees, this was considered the only accepted purpose of sculpture in the garden. In the country garden where the layout is more relaxed, such a use is now clearly inappropriate. Sculpture (and here I include any kind of informal sculptural ornament) is now more likely to be placed as a counterpoint to a fine tree or a good view, or as an interesting incident upon a terrace, for example. Alternatively, it can be positioned so as to create the centrepiece of its own enchanted world.

The forms of all the sculptural pieces below have a bold, simple outline, and properly sited they would add enormous interest to any garden.

Stone duck *This stone decoy duck sits in a bed of stonecrop and provides the sort of small incidental feature that brings a garden to life.*

Stone figure *The simple lines of this seated carved-stone figure are emphasized in silhouette against a green background.*

Discarded laundry mangle *An old white-painted mangle certainly provides a focal point of interest within the wild garden.*

Fibreglass figure *This contemplative sculpture (by Marion Smith) sits overlooking water and bog plants.*

Concrete doves *These two doves (by Marie Gill) sit upon a simple brick plinth. The accompanying plant is* Fatshedera lizei.

Attractive beehives *Beehives can provide a simple, sculptural, but practical element. This one stands behind a hydrangea.*

FEATURES

For many, the absence of the "enchanted" element in their garden (and this applies to town as well as country gardens) is immediately remedied by adding yet another decorative element, another urn or a Gothic summer-house. All this does is to shore up the deficiency visually when in fact the flaw is probably a much more fundamental design problem. "Stuck-on" decoration is rarely the solution for a garden that lacks something magical; what is necessary is an eye-catching feature that is truly part of the garden layout. If it has sculptural qualities too, so much the better.

You might have been lucky enough to have inherited some splendid, eye-catching feature with the garden you moved to. A dovecot such as the one in the picture below is an example, or it might be some topiary or a formal pool. In such cases, your task will be to integrate the feature into the garden layout that *you* (and your family) require, and to assess the planting that accompanies it. Remember that there will probably be annual maintenance to undertake.

As far as new features for the country garden are concerned, I suggest an extension of the natural garden approach, using local materials to make a decorative but functional addition, perhaps along the lines of the stone jetty, below on the opposite page. Its harmony with the garden and its surroundings would be ensured by the use of local stone for the steps down and the causeway to the water's edge. Of course there are many other options. Seating is important in any garden and its provision might well inspire you to create a special feature—an arbour perhaps, or a lookout.

Special places to sit (right) *A simple seat or sitting area, might be all that is required to create an enchanted feel within a garden. The trunk-encircling seat, far right, commands a glorious view through iron railings, while engendering its own strong sense of place. The inviting beech tree arbour, right, has been lovingly trained against an iron frame.*

Grand dovecot (below) *This dovecot is certainly not a decorative afterthought, it embellishes a large building, over a shady loggia.*

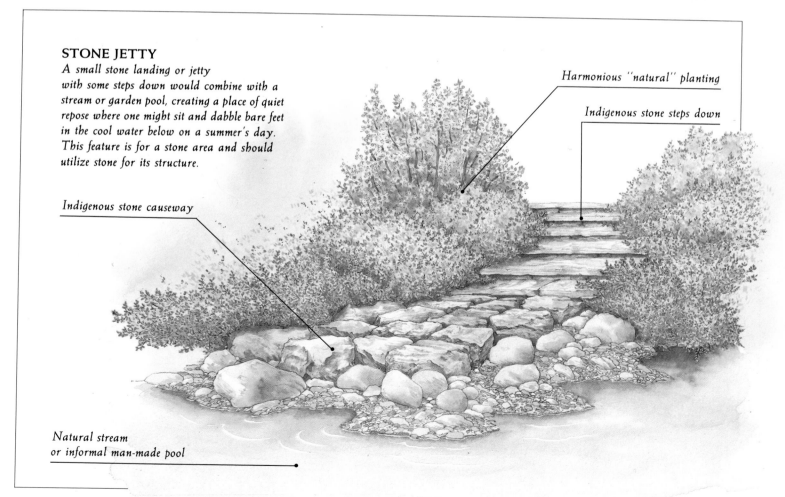

STONE JETTY

*A small stone landing or jetty
with some steps down would combine with a
stream or garden pool, creating a place of quiet
repose where one might sit and dabble bare feet
in the cool water below on a summer's day.
This feature is for a stone area and should
utilize stone for its structure.*

Harmonious "natural" planting

Indigenous stone steps down

Indigenous stone causeway

Natural stream
or informal man-made pool

THE GARDEN IN SUMMER

How selective memories of summer are. We usually only remember the pleasurable parts and these are invariably linked with the sun and fine weather—the times when you can sit outside for long lunches, or late into the evenings, bathed with a heady scent of honeysuckle, tobacco plants and lilies. The summertime garden is a totally sensuous experience, its scents and sounds combining to frame the joy of summer living. Now is the time to sunbathe, to potter, to pick and generally enjoy the fruits of your springtime labours, while tolerating the chores of grass cutting and watering in the cool stillness of the evening.

Rose blooms surely herald early summer and the increasing fullness of the garden, but it is not a particularly flowery time of the year among native plants since the first flush of blooms is over with spring. There are, however, musky scented phlox, asters and dahlias if you have a liking for them. It's the countryside beyond that is the most memorable thing about high summer—golden corn and stubble, picnics, and that peculiarly dull heaviness of surrounding tree foliage as it loses its spring freshness and creates deep pools of shadow.

There is a blanched look about the landscape if it has been hot and dry and flower colours have certainly strengthened, building to what will be their autumnal crescendo. Given moisture, gardens look full blown and things that have a mind to self-seed will have done so. Grasses are long and lush, and climbers rampant. Lushness describes much of the summer mood, and we live our lives outdoors in its full fruiting flood. Ponds, lakes and streams become irresistible attractions. Finally, the vigorous growth of the garden will need to be controlled and cut back in anticipation of the autumn tidy-up to come.

A fragrance of summer (right) *The perfume of lilies can be almost over-powering. Here they have been grown in pots for easy moving. The blue kingfisher daisy* (Felicia *sp.*) *is a half-hardy annual.*

A sound of summer (left) *The buzzing of bees is particularly evocative of summer. They love thistle heads, in this case* Eringium giganteum *'Miss Wilmot's Ghost'.*

SUMMER FRUITS

The soft and pitted fruits of summer can be a glorious bonus for the country gardener, from the earliest gooseberries—tough and reliable—to the treasured crops of sun-ripened strawberries. Some fruits, such as cherries, are an incidental bonus, whereas the berries are plants for the fruit garden and require special husbandry. Early, middle and late varieties spread the season to your requirements.

Blueberry
(Vaccinium corymbosum)
The bush thrives in acid, damp soil, and has attractive flowers and leaf colour

Cooking gooseberry
(Ribes uva-crispa *var.*)
Among the hardiest of soft fruits

Blackcurrant
(Ribes nigrum)
Bushes require warmth and protection

Dessert gooseberry (Ribes uva-crispa *var.*)
Need more time to ripen than cooking varieties

Red currant
(Ribes sativum)
Require similar conditions to gooseberries but with a sheltered site

Tay berry
(Rubus idaeus × fruticosus)
*A prolific cross between
blackberry and raspberry*

Raspberry
(Rubus idaeus *var.*)
*For the sunniest situation in the fruit
garden and traditionally grown on wires*

Wild strawberry
(Fragaria vesca)
*The little plants make a
decorative addition — their
fruit has great flavour*

Strawberry
(Fragaria *hybrids*)
*Essential for summer
desserts, strawberries
require a well-drained
patch in the fruit garden*

Sweet cherry
(Prunus avium)
*(two varieties)
Several trees must blossom
together for a usable crop*

ENJOYING THE SUNSHINE

Much of the joy of a country garden in summer is associated with sitting, eating and drinking in it. The vagaries of summer weather in many climes, however, along with morning and evening dews, often make the *fête champêtre*, a picnic on the ground, impossible. The answer is some form of seating which can be relaxed in, left out at night, and is tough enough for children to turn into an assault course. It is important too that seating is a feature in its own right, not a dominant one, but a feature none the less that harmonizes with its location.

The ideal country garden furniture is probably not painted white, is not metal and is certainly not smart. The chances are it is made of wood, which looks the part and is tough enough for the job. There are all kinds of wooden furniture that you can buy, while there is always the option of designing, and even constructing, your own, remembering that a relaxing seat is one that is generous and sturdy.

SIMPLE FURNITURE

My preference is for very simple wooden benches. Facsimilies of Sir Edwin Lutyens's celebrated bench designs are now easily obtainable, constructed in teak, oak, or cedar. The chairs and tables to match are similarly solid, comfortable and secure, but far from cheap. For many rural situations there is absolutely nothing wrong with re-using simple wooden kitchen chairs and a solid pine table, although treated with preservative. Close to the house these will be far more in character than the smartest "patio ensemble".

Half barrels (the coopered sort) of various sizes with bright splashes of annual colour growing in them look particularly good with timber furniture close to buildings. Choose a complementary colour scheme for your annuals in tubs and stick to it—the visual result will be much stronger than if you allow an ill-assorted colour mix.

Another visual delight, and enjoyable too, is the hammock. Slung between gnarled apple tress, its lazy presence is the confirmation of hot, high-summer days.

A summer's feast (right) *Black olives and blue vein cheese—ingredients for a summer lunchtime feast. Such delights look all the better against* Clematis 'Vyvyan Pennell'.

Shaded bench seat (below left) *A wooden bench and planted half-barrels look perfect in the country garden. The timber should be brushed down to remove mildew, and restained with preservative once a year.*

The potting table (below) *When the greenhouse becomes unbearably hot, an outdoor table for potting is a useful piece of furniture for a working corner of the garden.*

SALAD CROPS

Any country garden in summer can produce salad ingredients
of high quality to titillate the palate with their crisp freshness.
The decorative qualities of the growing plants are an
undoubted bonus.

Coriander (Coriander sativum)
*Use sparingly in strong-flavoured,
midsummer salads*

Chive (Allium
schoenoprasum)
*Adds a refreshingly
tangy bite to any salad*

Tomato (Lycopersicon
lycopersicum) *Small, sweet,
and full of health-giving vitamins*

Spring onion (Allium cepa)
*Picked young and tender for
both the bulb and leaves*

Fennel (Foeniculum
vulgare) *Striking aniseed-
flavoured plant*

Baby courgette
(Cucurbita pepo)
*Eaten when the fruit
is still unripe, after
removing the corolla*

Radish (Raphanus sativus)
*Refreshing, crisp mouthfuls
that require plenty of moisture
during growth*

Globe artichoke
(Cynara scolymus)
*A delectable vegetable
from a handsome plant*

Corn salad (Valerianella olitoria) *A small plant, but producing a useful quantity of leaves*

Oak-leaved lettuce (Lactuca sativa) *One of the attractive, crispy forms of leaf lettuce*

Radicchio (Cichorium intybus) *Has a similar tasty bitterness to chicory*

Endive (Cichorium endivia) *Has a stronger flavour than lettuce and is more hardy*

Asparagus (Asparagus officinalis) *Fleshy and tender spears, cut below ground level as they sprout above it*

Red-leaved lettuce (Lactuca sativa) *Crisp, curly-leaved variety with striking dark-red edging*

THE NEW BORDER

While a herbaceous perennial border can look superb, the work it demands is enormous considering how short a period it looks at its best. Incorporating woody plant material (shrubs and/or herbs) into the arrangement will give it much added interest and, if they are evergreen, extend the interest into other seasons as well. Include the odd climber on the fence or wall behind too and you will loosen up the regimented form of the border enormously and give it a more natural look.

Controlling the number of species in the new border, leaving room for bigger masses of what you do include, will make the effect as dramatic as possible. Your efforts will fail visually, however, unless the border is deep enough. If you intend including woody material anything under 2 m (6 ft) wide is too thin.

One of the characteristic features of such a mixed border is that it should appear to be so full that the material is overflowing. If the border abuts a lawn, it is best to lay a hard edging (brick or paving slabs) a fraction below the level of the lawn so that the bed can ooze on to that and not impede the mowing process. It is better still if your mixed planting abuts a gravel area, since you can plant some of the foreground species into the gravel itself (see p. 107) to extend the ooze. Small foreground stachys (that is the non-flowering variety *Stachys lanata* 'Silver Carpet'), feverfew and iris are good for this. Ideal smaller plants still include bugle (*Ajuga spp*), and varieties of *Allium*.

Effective use of strong summer colours (right) *In this mixed border, the strong summer yellows of achillea and verbascum, and reds of dahlias and nasturtiums, have maximum effect against a background of abundant green.*

When is a border a border? (below) *The hydrangea, rosemary and alchemilla grouping (left), and that of hebe, rheum and feverfew beneath an apricot (right), are both far from traditional summer borders, including sculptural form and bold masses.*

DAISY FLOWERS

Daisy-like blooms are, generally speaking, a pleasure of high and late summer in the country garden. They are mostly the flowers of herbaceous perennials, the main type of plant in the traditional herbaceous border, particularly species of the genus *Chrysanthemum*.

China aster (Callistephus chinensis) *The double-flowered form of this slightly tender annual*

Marguerites (Chrysanthemum frutescens) *Yellow- or white-flowering perennial, grown as an annual in colder climates*

Chrysanthemum indicum *'Snapper' Single type flower*

Chrysanthemum indicum *'Penny Lane' Single type flower*

Chrysanthemum indicum *Spoon type flower*

September flower *(Chrysanthemum sp.)* *produces a mass of tiny flowerheads in late summer*

Chrysanthemum indicum *'Carra' (right) Single type flower*

Chrysanthemum indicum *'Statesman' A mini pompon type*

Immortelle (Xeranthemum annuum) *An annual with flowers that will dry well for winter decoration*

Feverfew (Chrysanthemum parthenium) *Hardy perennial species that self-seeds freely*

Chrysanthemum indicum *'Rejour' (left) Single type flower*

China aster *(Callistephus chinensis) Semi-double form*

SUMMER COLOUR

It is a sad fact that much native flower colour will have spent itself by summer. Only in the perennial garden can you hope to sustain any sort of show, and even that is difficult in high summer if the planting is truly mixed and you are striving, in a limited area, to maintain a colour scheme. Planning for a display in a border devoted completely to high summer and autumn blooms is an easier matter, but interweaving flower interest for different seasons can be awkward. Particular plants are a great help, however, such as the sweetly-scented *Hosta plantaginea,* which retains its fresh green foliage when other hostas look tired, and produces white trumpet flowers very late in summer. A comparatively new variety of hosta called 'Honeybells' is related to it.

In the great traditional gardens of the early part of the century, the problem was overcome by either sinking pots of plants of particular interest for a period and then replacing them (using many gardeners) or interplanting perennials with annuals. The latter method is a useful technique for the modern country garden. A favourite of mine for this infill job is the tall white nicotiana, which smells so good at night. Its green cousin is also excellent.

Cool swathes of colour (right) *Massed delphiniums with* Rosa rubrifolia *form a backdrop to white* Aster *sp. with yellow* Lysimachia *sp. and* Centaurea *sp. in this display of cool summer colours.*

High summer flowers for decoration (below) *Larkspur, delphiniums, white helipterum and amaranthus can all be dried.*

OLD-FASHIONED ROSES

Unlike most modern roses, bred solely for showy blooms, old, shrub and some climbing roses, are hardy, low-maintenance shrubs with a host of visual attributes.

Rosa filipes 'Kiftsgate' (left)
Delicate, clustered blooms belie a rambling rose of great vigour

Chapeau de Napoleon
A centifolia rose

Ferdinand Pichard
A hybrid perpetual with striped globular blooms

James Mitchell (below)
Attractive "mossed" seedheads of this small-flowered, magenta-pink moss rose

Baby Fauras
Tiny polyantha rose, to 30cm (12in)

Gertrude Jekyll (above)
A new rose with rosette blooms and strong old rose fragrance

Souvenir du Dr Jamain (left)
A hybrid perpetual with double, deep cup blooms

The Portland Rose
A Damask rose, making a small bush

Rosa sericea pteracantha
A variety noted for its huge translucent thorns amongst ferny foliage

Zéphirine Drouhin (left)
*A Bourbon climbing rose
of exceptional fragrance*

**Rosa macrophylla
'Master Hugh'**
*Naturally occurring form with
some of the largest hips*

Louise Odier
*Exquisite Bourbon
rose with strong perfume
and bushy habit*

Blush Noisette
*An old climbing rose
of the noisette type,
for a warm wall*

Madame Isaac Pereire
*A tall, vigorously growing
Bourbon rose of great fragrance—
can be used as a climber*

Baroness Rothschild
*A hybrid perpetual rose,
with richly-scented, saucer
blooms in dense foliage*

The Fairy
*A polyantha rose, but its
habit is larger than the normal,
growing to a metre (3ft) high*

Gloire de Dijon
*This rose is a cottage garden
favourite of the noisette class,
with open-cupped blooms*

SUMMER TASKS

Summer is not just for relaxing outside. What seemed pristine at the end of spring quite quickly begins to look tired, and the spring-flowering species need cutting back to encourage a second flowering in autumn. Climbers need to be tied in or back as they grow; many of those seemingly casual arrangements of clematis clambering through this or that do in fact need some thought and manipulation from time to time. These are creative tasks that take but a minute of your time as you saunter in the garden.

But much of summer's labour is simply the mowing. The new country gardener is not troubled by the daily attentions involved in producing a lawn tennis court finish. But in a summer of some sun, some rain, where grass is the chief groundcover, mowing becomes a weekly chore, which has its rewards in the glorious smell of new-mown grass and the crisper look of the sward compared with the burgeoning growth elsewhere. By including areas of rough grass in the layout, which need cutting less often, some of the work can be reduced.

Watering may become another chore. The watering of newly-planted specimens may well start as early as mid-spring whenever there is a prolonged dry spell. Light, gravelly or sandy soils can dry out for months at a time in mid-summer, when a good soaking once a week will prolong the freshness of a garden enormously.

Creative lawn mowing (opposite) *This is an early summer display of dog daisies in rough grass on either side of a mown path. Such a lawn takes up to three years to establish from scratch.*

The ever-present hosepipe (below) *The device seen here, against the white froth of* Crambe cordifolia *flowers, is a sensible tidying post for that indispensible piece of summertime equipment, the hosepipe.*

GRASSES

There is infinitely more to grass in the country garden than a mown
lawn. This selection of elegant stems, leaves and seedheads was taken
from my garden in mid-summer and displays discreet qualities of shape,
texture and colour. All these specimens are easy to grow and
most are tolerant of indifferent soil.

Sedge (Carex morrowi variegata)
*Ideally suited to a partly-shaded
pool margin*

Purple moor-grass (Molina
caerulea variegata), right.
Tuft-forming perennial

Zebra-striped rush
(Miscanthus sinensis *'Zebrinus'*)
Attractive lateral stripes

Fescue (*Festuca
glauca*), below.

Creeping soft grass
(Holcus mollis), above.
*Variegated form of a perennial,
acid-loving grass*

**New Zealand
sedge** (Uncinia
unciniata) *A
visually-striking,
dark brown species*

Sedge (Carex stricta
'Bowles' Golden') Golden
*yellow form of this tender,
moisture-loving perennial*

Feather grass (Stipa variegata)
A metre-high (3-ft) form whose flower-heads glisten purple on opening

Feather grass (Stipa arundinaria)
Prefers a dry and sunny position and is useful in arrangements

Lyme grass (Elymus arenarius), right.
Vigorous in most soils although native of sandy habitats

THE WATER GARDEN

In the mind's eye, the perfect country garden has a natural stream coursing through its site, or has a pond with rushes, lily pads and ducks, to coincide with the lowest part of the garden where the water table naturally surfaces. But what of the majority of us whose gardens are not blessed with such idyllic features? Must we forego the inimitable sights and sounds of water and the undoubted contribution its presence makes in the country garden in terms of attracting wildlife of all sorts?

The answer, thankfully, is no, as long as your garden is not in a location where water would never establish itself naturally, such as a hill top. You can introduce water artificially, but its artificiality should not be apparent in the country garden. It is not the place for formal pools but rather for features that are, in some form or another, credible interpretations of naturally-occurring water.

PRACTICALITIES

It is tempting to try to reproduce the excitement of fast-moving natural water in the garden, a brook chattering over rocks with pools and eddies, or the languid, serpentine sweep of a lowland stream. Such a feature is extremely difficult to falsify on anything but a small scale, and requires resources and effort that contradict the relaxed, natural approach that the new country garden epitomizes. An informal area of still water, along the lines of the pool shown on page 157, is far more practical a proposition. Such a feature is so visually attractive that its presence will create the feel of the enchanted garden and it might therefore be sited in the intermediate zone of the garden (see p. 126), although the foremost requirement is a naturalistic site in a hollow.

Man-made but marvellous (right) *A natural-looking pool, such as this with its lilies, reeds, rushes, hemerocallis and eryngium, creates a feeling of instant tranquility.*

Natural water course (left) *A fast-moving stream in your garden is an all dominating feature that requires little gilding. Here ferns and iris are enough.*

NATURAL WATER

Should you be in the enviable position of having natural water within, running through, bordering or adjoining your garden, it will be very difficult to resist the temptation to garden its edges in a decorative way and generally "to make the most of it". Such a step can be a mistake, for, on the one hand, the natural beauty of the stream or pond will emphasize the man-made feel of the additions, and, on the other, the alien decoration will take the edge off the natural charm of the original. Nevertheless, you have a feature and want to exploit it.

The first step is to establish the essential character of the stream. Is it rocky and fast or mud-lined and sluggish? Notice how the force of water sculpts its containment, cutting into the bank on the outside of bends and leaving a beach on the inside. What about the nature of that beach—are its pebbles round or flat? The tallest planting will be at the back, getting smaller to the front of the newly established, dryer ground. You can extend and dramatize this natural look by planting in bold, simple groups and using strong plant form and leaf contrast.

Against this simple setting you might go on to introduce man-made features, the most obvious being the bridge. Keep the shape simple—there is no need for the Gothic nor Japanese styles when it comes to the basic form and/or the decoration of a bridge.

Chalk stream (right) *In chalk country, streams brim to the banks of their daisy-sprinkled banks. The rampant white rose 'Kiftsgate' strikes just the right level of decorative gardening in this example.*

Rocky-bedded stream (below) *In hard rock regions, streams rush along narrow, boulder-strewn courses making turns that create little beaches of pebbles. Their natural beauty needs no guilding.*

WATER FEATURES

Whereas in a town garden you might introduce the sound of running water perfectly adequately (trickling from a pipe through a wall, for example) using a modest electrical pump and a small cistern, the country equivalent of such a feature is on a much larger scale — the waterfall associated with a mill-pond, or the high drama of a natural waterfall. It is even possible (but difficult), in the self-contained world of a town garden, to re-create a section of a tiny brook, trickling over and through rocks; but how insignificant and inappropriate this would be in the country.

BUILDING A POOL

There is, however, a viable country-scale equivalent to the formal town garden pool, and that is a feature such as the natural-style pool shown in the plan below. It is a compromise between the completely wild pond and a cultivated garden pool, with approximately half of its perimeter retained by a low brick wall, while the remainder consists of earth bank or cobble beach. A mechanical excavator is needed for a pool of such dimensions (27.5 m (90ft) long by 1.5 m (5 ft) deep in its centre) before lining with sand and a heavy-gauge black, butyl-rubber liner. The retaining wall should be built on top of the liner. Some of the excavated earth can be pushed down into the pool (over the liner) and shaped to create a muddy area. The planting in this mud and on the bank behind, combined with the cobble beach and the sheet of still water itself, makes a strong feature.

Country scale (right) *The overflow from a mill-pond over a robust stone retaining wall, is now a purely decorative element in this garden. It is of a large enough scale to provide a powerfully attractive water feature.*

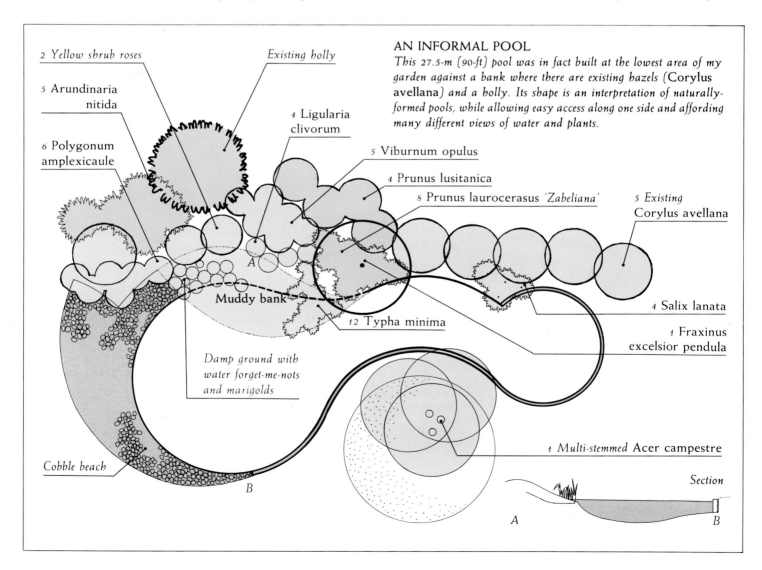

2 *Yellow shrub roses*

Existing holly

5 Arundinaria nitida

6 Polygonum amplexicaule

4 *Ligularia clivorum*

5 *Viburnum opulus*

4 *Prunus lusitanica*

8 *Prunus laurocerasus 'Zabeliana'*

5 *Existing Corylus avellana*

AN INFORMAL POOL
This 27.5-m (90-ft) pool was in fact built at the lowest area of my garden against a bank where there are existing hazels (Corylus avellana) and a holly. Its shape is an interpretation of naturally-formed pools, while allowing easy access along one side and affording many different views of water and plants.

A

Muddy bank

Damp ground with water forget-me-nots and marigolds

12 Typha minima

4 Salix lanata

1 Fraxinus excelsior pendula

Cobble beach

B

1 *Multi-stemmed* Acer campestre

A

Section

B

WATER PLANTING

The attraction of a mixed-planting group in association with water is due to the combination of strong leaf forms (often vertical) with the horizontal line of water itself. The added attractions of some colour and some insect life bring great potential for a marvellous addition to the country garden.

While most bog and waterside plants will flourish and are easy enough to care for once established, they have, in the main, very specific moisture requirements—some take any moist soil while others need to stand in up to 15 cm (6 in) of water. A great disadvantage is that few are evergreen, so the pond-side can look very bare in winter. Flowering tends to be from spring until early summer, after which the pond-side can look spent and drab. The secret therefore is to extend the period of interest over as long a summer time-span as possible through careful selection of water-loving plants.

Some of the earliest water plants to flower are the water buttercups (*Caltha palustris*) with water forget-me-nots (*Myosotis* sp.). Then come the flag iris (*Iris pseudoacorus*), followed by the early summer-flowering Japanese water iris (*Iris laevigata*). The wide range of primulas take over until, by late summer, the reeds and rushes (*Typha* sp.) produce their characteristic dark rounded poker flowers.

Water lilies will flower right through the period, until they are caught by the first frosts.

To sustain a natural look, waterside planting should not appear like a perennial flower border. Most natural waterside planting tends to consist of a single type of plant growing in a bold mass.

There is also a range of perennials and woody shrubs that look well growing in association with water, although this is not necessarily their original habitat. I am particularly fond of the shrubby willows and dogwoods (see pp.58-59)—their coloured stems are marvellous for winter interest.

Arum lily (right) *The white spathes of the arum lily (*Zantedeschia aethiopica*) show up well against the enormous leaves of* Gunnera manicata. *The foreground plants growing in the water are arrowheads (*Sagittaria *sp.), whose foliage is indispensable for a natural planting.*

Flags and loosestrife (below left) *The white flag (*Iris pseudacorus alba*), yellow loosestrife (*Lysymachia punctata*) and, on the left,* Rodgersia *sp. make this lovely and colourful plant combination for a pool-side situation.*

Early flowering marsh marigold (below) *The single yellow marsh marigold (*Caltha palustris*) is one of the earliest flowering aquatic plants. There are many other forms of it, including double and white.*

THE SHADE GARDEN

While in many countries summer shade is a prized commodity, throughout much of the gardened world people bemoan it, saying that little will grow there. And being discouraged by shade is an urban complaint as well as a rural one. It is true that there are a few forest trees beneath which little will grow—beeches, horse chestnuts and mature conifers in particular—but the shade of which gardeners complain is more often that cast by a building or a wall, or the dappled shade caused by trees and shrubs of lesser size. The density of shade caused by tree foliage can be altered by thinning their heads, changing deep shade to medium or medium to light. Thinning is quite different to cutting back, since the aim is to *retain* the overall size of the tree but to reduce its thickness. This you achieve by removing selected boughs in winter, when the tree's sap is low (it is advisable to have a tree surgeon undertake the work). Light shade can be turned to advantage simply by choosing from the many plants that thrive in shady conditions.

SHADE-TOLERANT PLANTS
Many of the plants that enjoy shade have gradually adapted themselves to life in reduced light by developing large leaves. Visually, this characteristic makes them very attractive material to plant; the many forms of hosta are a fine example. The flower colour of shade-loving specimens tends to be pale, however.

There is also a whole range of ground-covering plants that is excellent for semi-shade conditions, plants such as *Vinca* sp. or *Rubus tricolor,* which will even become too rampant. So far from being a disadvantage, a shaded area can become very attractive.

Semi-shaded glory (right) Alchemilla mollis, *with* Polygonum *and* Angelica *sp. make up the perennial ground-cover of this semi-shaded area.*

Autumnal shade (left) Cyclamen neapolitanum *will form a dainty carpet. The marbling of the leaves is as attractive a feature as the flowers themselves.*

SHADE PLANTING

Shade with moisture provides ideal growing conditions for many plants, dappled shade being the best. As long as your soil is not alkaline, such conditions provide the natural habitat for all the rhododendrons and azaleas and also for camellias and acers. The plants for shade with a chalky soil are fewer, but *Aucuba japonica* (a much maligned plant) and its relative *Prunus laurocerasus*, the laurel, with many of the viburnums, will do well in such conditions.

Smaller shrubs for shade and most soil types belong to the genera *Rhus, Elaeagnus, Hamamelis, Helleborus and Hydrangea*. The elders (*Sambucus* spp.) are excellent, quick-growing shrubs for the semi-wild look. The range

Water cistern feature (right) *The gentle lady fern* (Athyrium filix-femina) *makes an attractive incident on the shady side of a decorative water cistern.*

Flower colour for shade (opposite) *The orange lily flowers of* Crocosmia *sp., against the deep green of ferns, make a dramatic counterpoint to naturalized, blue-flowering hydrangeas in damp, acid soil.*

Solomon's seal (below) *Solomon's seal* (Polygonatum multiflorum) *has both attractive arching branches of foliage and cream-scented flowers hanging from the axils.*

includes variegated and cut-leaf forms that have great charm. For groundcover *Vinca* spp. are excellent — *Vinca minor* being a tidier plant than *Vinca major*.

PLANTS FOR DRY SHADE

The dry shaded area is rather more difficult to cope with horticulturally than is the damp shaded one. Dry shade is usually found in association with buildings, where the soil is often clay because of its suitability as a base for foundations.

Bamboos (*Arundinaria* spp.) are excellent in this situation, but they do not like wind. The *Berberis* genus, along with mahonias and cotoneasters, are great stand-bys. Species of *Skimmia* are also shrubs that tolerate dry shade and make excellent components for the framework of a planting scheme. For groundcover use ajuga (which is good in dry and damp shade), bergenia and euonymous.

Shaded waterside site (right) *Growing in the shade of both a Japanese and a field maple, is a mass of scaly male ferns* (Dryopteris pseudomas). *The pale points of colour are wild balsam and a low, cream-flowering* Hydrangea quercifolia.

White anemones (below) *The white-flowering Japanese anemone* (Anemone japonica alba) *is a captivating plant, providing late summer interest in light shade.*

THE WORKING GARDEN

The only sort of country garden for many is the working garden. They enjoy the satisfaction of producing fresh fruit and vegetables for the table and the noble art of cultivation that goes with it. They may even be tempted by the wholesome advantages of self-sufficiency.

However, many of us now find that just as our cherished crops are ready for picking, so are those at the local "pick-your-own". So the new working garden might be put to better use by growing a more limited but special range of vegetables and fruit. A range perhaps inspired by culinary requirements, including crops that are always a treat to the palate, such as asparagus tips or globe artichokes.

THE SOIL
With purely decorative gardening you can turn the nature of your site and soil to advantage, choosing a style and range of plants that complements it, whether it be exposed and sandy or shaded and damp. However, the nature of the soil, how much there is of it, and whether or not it receives plenty of growth-inducing sunshine, are decisive factors when it comes to the working garden.

A light sandy soil is the easiest, since it warms up and dries out quickly in spring and is relatively easy to work. But its open, fast-draining texture means it will require regular feedings or it will lose its fertility rapidly. The chalky soils that occur over gravel have a "sweetness" (alkalinity) that produces good vegetables. Heavy clay soils are cold and difficult to break up, since they dry out so late after winter. When well-fed and conditioned, they will nevertheless produce excellent crops.

Healthy beauty (right)
The celebrated vegetable garden at Barnsley House, in Gloucestershire, has all the wholesome ingredients of the working garden combined with obvious charm.

Food with good looks (left) *The wide range of attractive cabbage forms includes slow-growing, crinkly savoys, and varieties of the common cabbage with pink-tinged veins.*

USING FOOD CROPS DECORATIVELY

The dramatic planting in the beautiful, church-side garden below, is solely of culinary crops. Crispy-leaved parsley grows in front of the majestic foliage of globe artichokes, which, in turn give way to an explosion of feathery asparagus. More and more, gardeners are recognizing the visual attributes of vegetables and fruit, and including them in general mixed plantings of shrubs and perennials.

This is increasingly done in smaller gardens, where there is not enough space for a separate kitchen garden.

The idea is not so novel when you consider the now well-established decorative uses of culinary herbs. To these you can add maize, ornamental cabbages (for wonderful winter colour and form) and species of the genus *Rubus* (blackberry) purely for their looks.

Blackcurrant *Not quite so spectacular as its redcurrant cousin, blackcurrants are still a useful addition to any fruit garden.*

Trained fruit *Fruit trees trained over a path create a fascinating tunnel effect whether bare-stemmed, in flower, or in fruit.*

Redcurrant *Though an insignificant plant for much of the year, the redcurrant in fruit provides a bright splash of summer colour.*

Lettuce varieties *Rank upon rank of different lettuce varieties produces a subtle blend of visual and tactile effects.*

Onions *Rows of onions prior to their harvesting at the end of summer make an interesting abstract pattern on the ground.*

Light greens *Not a flower in sight, but the quality of light reflected by the leaves of French beans, lettuce and leeks is stunning.*

Florence fennel *The extraordinary fan-shaped bulbous stems of Florence fennel are topped with typical fern-like foliage.*

Winter cabbage *There is a vast range of plants in the brassica family, none more sumptuous than the good old winter cabbage.*

Ruby chard *The scarlet stems of ruby chard provide spectacular late summer colour when massed within a mixed planting.*

LIVESTOCK

For those with a garden too large to manage, the idea of keeping some sheep, a donkey or some geese to keep the grass down can sound like a simple answer. But it is all too easy to swop one set of gardening problems for another of the two or four-legged kind. Any livestock needs containment, supervision and management, so it is probably best to seek the co-operation of a friendly farmer to see if he will put his animals on your land. He might be pleased of a little extra grazing for some sheep, for example. Of course you must make sure that your fencing is adequate to keep the animals from straying on to roads, but the responsibility for the stock remains the farmer's.

There are many parents who have given way to their children's request for a pony, thereby involving themselves in a great responsibility, not only to the poor animal but to the community at large. The semi-suburban areas on the perimeter of most large towns now have acres of dissipated substandard grazing, ill-fenced, mismanaged and cluttered with unsound structures in which unfortunate animals survive, often loved, but in fact neglected through ignorance.

However, there are others who are interested in and concerned about their stock, many of whom are doing valuable work in saving rare breeds of domestic cattle, pigs, sheep and fowl. Such animals do not have a direct commerical value nowadays, but their unique genetic patterns are a valuable resource that deserves saving.

Half the point of keeping livestock is to see and enjoy it, so some manipulation of fencing boundaries, or removal of shrubbery, may be necessary to bring shelters and runs into the overall garden concept. It may be seen against the backdrop of surrounding landscape (and even be an extension of its mood) or it might somehow be incorporated into the transitional zone of the garden layout (see Zone B on p.28).

Any sort of livestock is a huge responsibility on a number of levels and its maintenance should not be considered lightly.

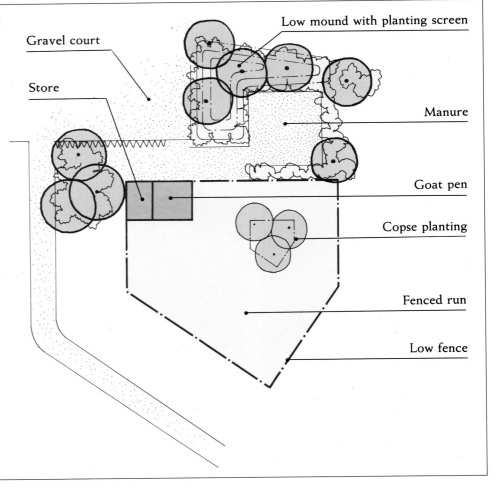

INTEGRATED LIVESTOCK PEN

My own particular livestock fantasy is to keep a small herd of pygmy goats, whose liveliness and charm I find totally captivating. I have just the place for them, with access to their small shelter and ample storage area off a hard parking area. Their run must be low-fenced and encompasses about 20 metres square (⅛ acre). Some standard trees (fenced for protection) will afford the goats some shade and shelter. Behind their pen is a screened area for composting their manure.

Gravel court

Store

Low mound with planting screen

Manure

Goat pen

Copse planting

Fenced run

Low fence

Goats *All goats have great character, but they need permanent weatherproof shelter and supervision since they should not be left outside in cold conditions, in the rain or overnight.*

Ducks *Not only are ducks such as these Buff Orpingtons the perfect visual complement to a pond or stream, but they also provide eggs and meat for the kitchen table.*

Free-ranging hens *There is something very comforting about having some hens about the place. Allowing them free range is ideal, although they should be limited by netting.*

Cows *A neighbouring farmer might agree to using your land as extra grazing. Prize Jersey cows such as these, however, are likely to remain a visual delight on his side of the fence.*

STORE BUILDINGS

For the practical country gardener, the store shed is rather like the kitchen of a traditional home—it is the place where all the important day-to-day functions happen. It deserves to be ordered, to provide a practical, dry store for expensive tools that need maintenance and cleaning after use. Lawn mowers in particular need constant care if they are not to give up on you.

It is items like canes, stakes and hoses that clutter a storage space very quickly. My particular aversion is the new type of plastic hose that twists and does not roll up neatly! There is also the evergrowing mountain of flower pots we can't bear to throw away. The terracotta pots feel so nice, and will probably become collectors' items soon. Then there are the unfinished sacks of this and that, compost or bonemeal for instance. Ideally they need their own bins. But more important is the safe storage of lethal sprays and weedkillers, which should be stored high and locked up, away from children and/or pets.

LOGS FOR FUEL

The wise countryman buys in—or saves up his wood a year in advance, keeping it neatly stored and drying out for the following winter. If he is really smart he buys in kindling wood, intermediate-size logs and then hefty Yule-tide ones, and stores them separately. He should also have pinned up nearby the following lines to remind him of the qualities of the different woods he can burn.

Beechwood fires are bright and clear, if the logs are kept a year;
Oaken logs burn steadily, if the wood is old and dry.
Chestnut's only good, they say, if for long it's laid away.
But ash new or old
Is fit for a Queen with a crown of gold.

Birch and fir logs burn too fast—blaze up bright, but do not last.
Make a fire of elder tree, death within your house you'll see.
It is by the Irish said hawthorn bakes the sweetest bread.
But ash green or ash brown
Is fit for a Queen with a golden crown.

Elm wood burns like churchyard mould—e'en the very flames
are cold.

Poplar gives a bitter smoke, fills your eyes and makes you choke.
Apple wood will scent your room, with an incense-like perfume.
But ash wet or ash dry
For a Queen to warm her slippers by.   *(Author unknown)*

Open-sided shelter (right) *Traditional tools are beautiful and this open-sided tool store makes a real feature of them.*

Tool shed extension (below) *A small open barn built as an extension to a tool shed makes a useful all-purpose store.*

THE HERB GARDEN

Herbs, particularly their medicinal properties, have been written about since Roman times, but not until the late twentieth century have they received quite so much attention. Perhaps this is in reaction to their rejection during the nineteenth century and the early part of this one, in favour of newly discovered "scientific" medications. None of the properties of herbs advocated for generations has changed, but since we are now concerned about taking too much synthetic chemical into our bodies, we have turned to the medicinal, culinary, cosmetic and oderiferous qualities of herbs with a new vengeance.

INFORMAL USE OF HERBS

Think of the herb garden, and many are drawn to the idea of formal schemes, including knot gardens, where herbs have to be constantly tended and clipped to maintain intricate patterns. Although these can be successful when linked to a grand and formal building, there is no requirement to use herbs in this way. Such a usage is in the tradition of the enclosed garden that turns its back on nature.

Many gardeners include herbs amongst their plantings quite unconsciously—rosemary for instance, lavender, rue, many of the grey-leaved plants and so on. But the new-look country garden does not include such time-consuming features as herbaceous borders; rather, it uses all its plants, including herbs, in a far less conscious manner. There are plants for scent that you brush against, chamomiles to walk upon, and groupings that will attract insects and butterflies. Then there is the culinary collection of herbs, planted in pleasing combinations both by the kitchen door, and amongst your vegetables.

Shropshire herb garden
(right) *Chives (*Allium schoenoprasum*), one of the smallest of the onion family, are massed together in this garden.*

Herby window-sill
(left) *This herbal harvest includes garlic cloves, rosemary and thyme, and marinating herbal vinegars. The little bundles are home-made* bouquet garni.

THE VERSATILITY OF HERBS

Herbs growing as companion plants to other food crops may well have a beneficial effect while they are growing. One theory suggests that certain herbal scents, root excretions and other plants exhalations will deter insect pests. It is a fact that herbs themselves are seldom attacked by them. Nasturtiums, for instance, are said to deter aphids, while tansy and southernwood ward off fruit moth, and garlic and other alliums protect most garden plants from a variety of pests. Wormwood and rue are even said to discourage animal pests such as slugs and moles. By considering carefully which plants to grow together, you can promote healthy growth, using a completely natural form of pest control.

NATURAL DYES

There is a range of herbs that provide natural dyes of a depth and lustre that no synthetic dye can match (woad for blue, for example, madder for red and chamomile for yellow). Wool is the preferred fibre for natural dyes as it achieves an even take; some country gardeners dye the wool from their own paddock sheep. However, other natural fibres, such as cotton and linen, also colour well so growing herbs for dying is doubly worthwhile.

Biennial herbs *Woad* (Isatis tinctoria, *foreground), is an ancient blue dye plant, while angelica (*Angelica archangelica, *behind) may be used in several dishes for flavouring fish.*

Sweet cicely (Myrrhis odorata) *The stems of sweet cicely can be chopped up and stewed with fruit as a sugar substitute. The seeds of the plant can also be used as a flavouring—they taste of liquorice.*

Thyme (Thymus *sp.*) *The most common of the aromatic herbs, thyme is used particularly with Mediterranean food. Its pungency blends with garlic, olives, tomatoes and the wines of Southern cuisine.*

Parsley (Petroselinum crispum) *There are many forms of parsley—this is the curled-leafed form that is so useful for garnishes and in salads. Its flavour is subtler than that of French parsley (see p.183).*

Dill (Anethum graveolens) *Dill is a hardy annual. The leaves are used in much Scandinavian cooking, particularly with fish, while its seeds taste of caraway and are used for seasoning.*

Sage (Salvia officinalis) *Sage tends to be overused with fatty foods, but is excellent with sausage meat and as a flavouring with cheeses (Derby and Vermont). An infusion makes a good gargle for a sore throat.*

Chamomile (Chamaemelum nobile) *Chamomile is useful as a grass substitute for lawns. A non-flowering form, C.h. 'Treneague', is best for lawns as the species chamomile needs to be de-flowered.*

HERB PLANTING

Herbs will grow in most soils, as long as they are in full sun. The selection becomes restricted if your soil is extremely acid or alkaline, but if it is generally poor, take heart; herbs prefer this to a rich soil. There is a limited range of herbs for damp and shady positions.

For normal household culinary use your herbs need to be close to hand, combining quite large numbers of some plants, but only a few of others. It depends on your cooking. For myself a little sage goes a very long way, while I use masses of chives, sorrel, basil, tarragon, parsley and mint.

You may plant up these masses in blocks or grow them in a random manner. Intersperse them with the odd rosemary or even a shrub rose and your culinary bed instantly becomes decorative. To extend the decorative content, consider the contrasting colours of herb foliage that you might incorporate. There are the golds of varieties of marjoram, feverfew, thyme and sage, and then the much larger range of silver- and grey-leaved plants, the artemisias, lavenders and mints, and also sage, rue and santolina. The final ingredient should be tones of purple foliage, choosing from bronze fennel, purple sage, black peppermint, and purple basil.

Herb garden in autumn *The herb garden in autumn is past its best, but late summer sun illuminates the foliage colours and textures of purple sage (foreground), with rosemary beyond.*

HERB PLANTING SCHEME

This is a planting scheme for a small herb garden, outside the kitchen door, next to the sunniest corner of a house. The terrace is of stone slab with a brick paver infill, and occasional stone slabs are positioned throughout the garden from which to pick. Big masses of useful culinary herbs are mixed with more decorative shrubby ones, so that the mixture has form and interest through the year. The herbs are allowed to run off into the gravel surround at the outer edges of the garden. Mints are restricted to pots since they are so invasive.

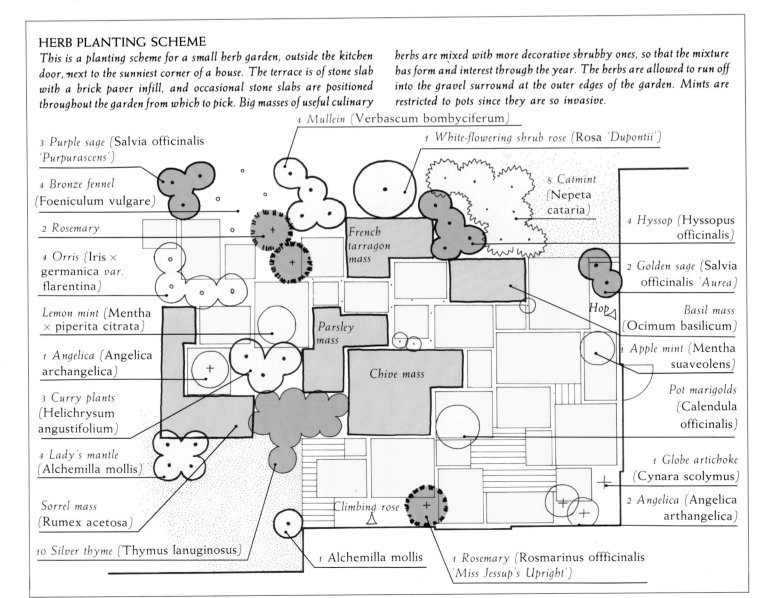

3 *Purple sage* (Salvia officinalis 'Purpurascens')

4 *Bronze fennel* (Foeniculum vulgare)

2 *Rosemary*

4 *Orris* (Iris × germanica *var.* flarentina)

Lemon mint (Mentha × piperita citrata)

1 *Angelica* (Angelica archangelica)

3 *Curry plants* (Helichrysum angustifolium)

4 *Lady's mantle* (Alchemilla mollis)

Sorrel mass (Rumex acetosa)

10 *Silver thyme* (Thymus lanuginosus)

4 *Mullein* (Verbascum bombyciferum)

1 *White-flowering shrub rose* (Rosa 'Dupontii')

8 *Catmint* (Nepeta cataria)

French tarragon mass

Parsley mass

Chive mass

Climbing rose

1 *Alchemilla mollis*

1 *Rosemary* (Rosmarinus offficinalis 'Miss Jessup's Upright')

4 *Hyssop* (Hyssopus officinalis)

2 *Golden sage* (Salvia officinalis 'Aurea')

Hop

Basil mass (Ocimum basilicum)

1 *Apple mint* (Mentha suaveolens)

Pot marigolds (Calendula officinalis)

1 *Globe artichoke* (Cynara scolymus)

2 *Angelica* (Angelica arthangelica)

THE GARDEN IN AUTUMN

Autumn is a time of action in the country garden. Just as in nature all is gathered and stored for winter use, so in the garden the summer crops are harvested, and flowers hung up to dry. Logs are sawn, jams are made and the garden tidied and virtually "put to bed" for winter. It is a season of satisfaction for the job well done, completed against the honeyed background of harvested fields.

As the plough follows the harvester, the country-gardener follows the harvest by digging, so that frost action can have its beneficial effect on the soil, and compost spreading amongst the shrubs to feed and shelter their roots through the coming winter months.

PLANNING AND PLANTING

Autumn is also the time for planning and planting, not just the spring bulbs but also trees and shrubs. These days, when we buy most new plants container-grown and ready for planting at any time of year, as long as the ground is neither frost bound nor gripped by drought, we tend to forget that autumn is the traditional time for planting shrubs and trees. At one time larger plants were dug for you by the grower (sometimes this is still the case with trees) and at this time of year the exposed and cut roots had the best chance of recovery. For this reason autumn is still the best time for repositioning a youthful shrub, or even moving a tree, especially if you have prepared it a month or so beforehand, using a spade to partially isolate from the surrounding earth the largest amount of earth you can move with the specimen.

Gardening is a transitory craft, and in autumn the anticipation of next year's scene is a spur to improve on the results of the summer past.

Autumn labours (left) *Autumn is the time for cutting back, burning or composting the spent season's growth, and rationalizing what remains.*

The last blooms of summer (right) *Autumn sunlight has a unique glowing quality that here illuminates foreground penstemon against the bold leaves of* Viburnum rhytidophyllum.

HERBS FOR DRYING

Here is a selection of herbs, some freshly picked, others dried, all of which can be grown in the country garden. They are beautiful plants for inclusion in a decorative, mixed planting scheme, but they are also invaluable in the home. Their cultivation could not be easier—most like to be hot and dry.

Bay (Laurus nobilis) *Use dried for flavouring, individually and in bouquet garni*

Tarragon (Artemisia dracunculus)

Basil (Ocimum basilicum 'Minimum') *For salads, sauces and cheeses*

Chives (Allium shoenoprasum) *A classic component of* fines herbes

Rosemary (Rosmarinus officinalis) *Use particularly with lamb*

Sage (Salvia officinalis) *Use in stuffings and cheeses. Infuse purple sage (S.o.'Purpurascens') for a throat gargle*

Thyme (Thymus sp.) *Use the leaves of woody thymes in bouquet garni and for general seasoning*

Dill (Anethum graveolens) *Use this feathery annual with salad and pickle, fish and poultry*

Pot marjoram (Origanum onites) *Leaves used to season meat and vegetables*

German chamomile (Matricaria chamomilla) *Use the dried flowers to make a calming tea*

French sorrel (Rumex scutatus) *For soups, salads and sauces*

Chervil (Anthriscus cerefolium) *A substitute for parsley and good with egg dishes*

French parsley (Carum petroselinum) *Stronger flavour than common parsley*

Bouquet garni *Parsley stalks, sprigs of thyme and marjoram, and a bay leaf, all in a twist of muslin*

Coriander (Coriander sativum) *Include in soups and stews*

THE ESSENCE OF AUTUMN

The passing of the autumnal equinox is the prelude to strong sidelight as the sun's daily path sinks towards the horizon. The details of the garden are brought into high relief, shadows are longer and leaves and stems are back-lit. In the evenings, falling temperatures make a fire a welcome thing again. The wider gap between day and night temperatures makes dews heavy, covering every detail in crystal droplets.

The gardener's presence is often denoted by spires of grey smoke rising out of the greenery, for it is time to burn up the summer surpluses of spent growth and the first fallen leaves. Asters gleam in low sunlight, and dahlia blooms ignore the countdown to the first night frost. All sad in a way, but it is a time of blackberry picking, of russety bracken, and swathes of heather upon the moor.

Heavy dews and long shadows *Autumn is a poignant time of dew-dropped cob-webs in the early mornings (right) and long afternoon shadows (below).*

Orchard tidy (opposite) *With summer's growth over, tidying can start, including cutting back and grubbing out if necessary.*

APPLES

The apple tree (*Malus sylvestris*), in its multifarious varieties
that bear fruits pleasing to both the eye and the palate, is hardly
ever out of place in a country garden. Saplings are a joy to nurture,
while gnarled old beauties are to be treasured.

Baker's Delicious *Pick when
orange-red flush appears. Maintains
its flavour for about three weeks
and requires gentle handling*

St Edmund's Russet
*Crisp and juicy, maintaining its
distinctly russet flavour
for about three weeks*

Red Ellison *Keeps crisp for a
fortnight, then mellows, developing
a strong aniseed scent and flavour*

Worcester Pearmain *A properly
ripe Worcester is half bright red,
sweet and crunchy. Best picked
as required*

Queen Cox *A richly
coloured and flavoured
type of Cox that lasts a full
three months after picking*

Lobo *The deep red skin contrasts
with a white juicy flesh of meringue-
like texture. Ideal for salads,
baking and sauce*

Sunset *Juicy, but a
solid, "meaty" apple with
a rich, tangy flavour
and characteristic sunset-
like colouring*

Ribston Pippin *Reputed to be a
parent of the Cox apple, with a
strong, spicy flavour that develops
with the brick-red flush, and matures
through the winter*

Orleans Reinette *A large, spicy russet apple that flushes orange when ripe in late autumn. Rich, nutty flavour with a grainy texture*

Cornish Gilliflower *Conspicuously ribbed. Pick as maroon flush develops for delicious, crisp, sweet, full-bodied eating*

Michaelmas Red *Deep red skin and tender white flesh that is juicy and mildly sweet. Small unless thinned in early summer*

Warner's King (Cooking) *At its best in early winter. Good for apple dumplings*

Arthur Turner (Cooking) *Pick the largest weekly from high summer to early winter. An excellent baker*

'Merton Joy *A showy, mid-season apple. Crisp and fairly sharp as it ripens, but quickly mellows as it develops a vague spicy flavour*

Monarch (Cooking) *Slightly "dented" all over its shiny surface. Excellent for mincemeat and good for grilling*

Woolbrook Russet (Cooking) *A dull green, acid cooker that is as versatile as a Bramley. Its Russet skin wrinkles through the winter*

Bramley (Cooking) *This celebrated apple is not invariably green, it sometimes sports a cheerful crimson flush. Susceptible to frost damage*

AUTUMN COLOUR

The intensity of autumn colour alters from year to year according to the weather (a sharp fall in temperature producing a more fleeting but more brilliant foliage display) and from region to region depending on the nature of the location and its soil. On acid soils, for example, reds are particularly deep, while on chalk, the leaves of field maples and *Sorbus* sp. have a much yellower look. In general, autumn colour in the north of England is far more subtle with the delicate golds of birches and purple patches upon the moors predominating.

COLOURED FRUITS

Much of the richness of autumnal colour is provided by fruit—not necessarily the edible kind, although a heavily laden apple orchard with autumn sun upon it is a sight to behold and worth a place in any country garden.

Amongst smaller decorative garden trees, varieties of Mountain ash (*Sorbus aucuparia*) provide a whole range of coloured berries from the pink/white ones of *S.a.* 'Cashmiriana', through the yellow and amber of *S.a.* 'Joseph Rock', to the scarlet of *S.a.* 'Matsumurana', the Japanese mountain ash. Then there are the delightful fruits of crab apples, the *Malus* genus. *Malus* 'Gold Hornet' fairly glows until mid-winter, while the orange/scarlet, conical fruits of *Malus* 'John Downie' make wonderful jelly. *Malus* 'Red Sentinel' produces massive clusters of cardinal red fruit that last through to spring.

Viburnums, pyracantha and cotoneasters together provide a huge range of berry colours and tones (blues, oranges, reds and yellows), on shrubs or climbing plants that will suit many country locations.

Late autumn sunlight (right) *Here, late autumn sunlight falls on a row of poplars with a hornbeam (*Carpinus *sp.) hedge glowing beyond. Like beech, hornbeam retains its leaves in winter.*

Side light (below left) *It is the strong light from the autumn sun that throws colour into strong relief against deep shade. Here, an aged beech gives way to a sun-drenched mass of shrubs.*

Orange-berried pyracantha (below) Pyracantha *spp. the firethorn, is a close relative of the many varieties of cotoneaster. All are laden with white flowers in early summer and then have the bonus of spectacularly coloured berries in autumn.*

HARVEST VEGETABLES

If anything is to inspire the gourmet within us, it is surely an array of vegetable garden produce such as this, beautiful at harvest time, when growing, and in the pot. The kitchen garden is a place where you can fuse decorative with practical gardening.

Jerusalem artichoke (Helianthus tuberosus) *Tasty tubers that make fine soup*

Salsify (Tragopogon porrifolius) *Known as vegetable oyster, owing to the taste of the cooked roots*

Sweet corn (Zea mays) *To be planted in blocks of short rows for both looks and fertilization*

Beetroot (Beta vulgaris) *A vegetable or salad crop, the globe-rooted form being most useful*

Turnip (Brassica rapa) *A purple-top variety, picked young for its tender flesh*

Carrot (Daucus carota) *A slender, tapering variety for use raw or cooked*

Onion (Allium cepa) *Two varieties from the several classes of an indispensible vegetable*

Field mushroom (Psalliota campestris) *A tasty bonus that accompanies misty autumnal mornings*

Kohl-rabi (Brassica oleracea caulorapa) *Requires moisture during growth*

Purple broccoli (Brassica oleracea italica) *Crops through autumn and into winter*

Calabrese (Brassica oleracea italica) *Less hardy than purple broccoli, but more flavourful*

Round zucchini (Cucurbita pepo) *A vegetable of great culinary versatility*

Celeriac (Apium graveolens rapaceum) *Tasty turnip-rooted celery*

Pumpkin (Cucurbita maxima), (right), *and* **squash** (C. pepo cv.) *Best used young, like marrow*

Marrow (Cucurbita pepo) *Best cut when small to medium in size*

AUTUMN TIDY-UP

Long before autumn is officially over, many garden tasks seem very wintery. The general sweep, clean and burn up, for instance, and the spreading and light forking through of compost or well-rotted farmyard manure. It is the best time for sorting and moving many plants, dividing them where necessary. The temptation is to leave the job until spring but by then herbaceous perennials will be unrecognizable, if showing at all.

Only cut back those shrubs that are truly hardy in your region. Last year's straggling growths (of established lavenders for instance) will help to protect plants from heavy frosts through winter.

Dividing perennials (right) *When dividing plants use two forks to prize apart fibrous perennial root masses. If this fails, or if the root is tuberous take a spade and chop it through.*

Autumn bonfires (below) *Bonfire time in the orchard is all part of the autumn tidy-up. Your overall aim should be to create the neat put-to-bed look of a winter garden.*

GARDEN
CASE HISTORIES

*The plans shown on the following pages
represent a number of my designs for country gardens. The
purpose of one of them (see p. 195) is to introduce new country
style to a town plot for a relaxed, easy-to-maintain look.
The remainder, in country locations, display a host of
problems that commonly occur and can be solved in many
different ways to suit the requirements of the garden's users.
You may find some inspiration here when it comes
to planning your own layout.*

ADDING PRIVACY TO A GARDEN

One problem facing this large garden was a lack of privacy. On the north side of the cottage there is a charming view up a reach of stream with a public right of way on its opposite bank. The south side of the cottage borders a road. The front door was rarely used since the only access to it was via a small path leading from the road. The kitchen door on the east side was used instead. The new garden has been redirected away from the stream towards a beautiful meadow full of flowers. A new yew hedge screens the garden from the road and forecourt, while the public right of way beyond the stream to the north is hidden by

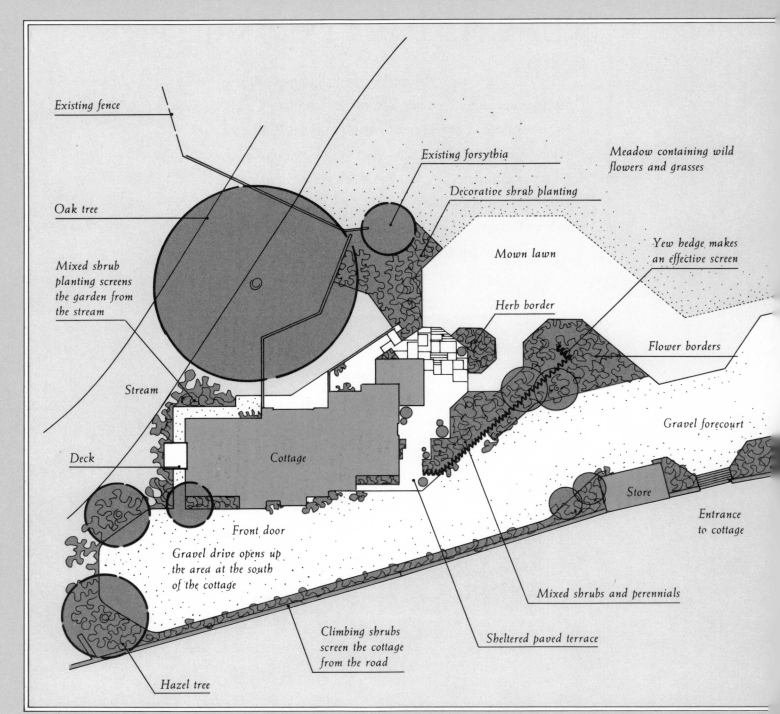

Existing fence

Existing forsythia

Meadow containing wild flowers and grasses

Oak tree

Decorative shrub planting

Mixed shrub planting screens the garden from the stream

Yew hedge makes an effective screen

Mown lawn

Herb border

Flower borders

Stream

Deck

Cottage

Gravel forecourt

Store

Front door

Entrance to cottage

Gravel drive opens up the area at the south of the cottage

Mixed shrubs and perennials

Climbing shrubs screen the cottage from the road

Sheltered paved terrace

Hazel tree

TOWN GARDEN

shrub planting. A gravel drive has been added along the south side of the house to allow access to the front door, and a vegetable garden is now located away from the house, screened by a box hedge.

The requirements for this small town garden are that it should involve little maintenance and look spacious. It has been redesigned to incorporate a new but "distressed" natural look. The lawn has been replaced with a stone-paved terrace and different levels of gravel containing random planting. Large stepping stones link the areas. A partially concealed grassy play area has been created at the bottom of the garden.

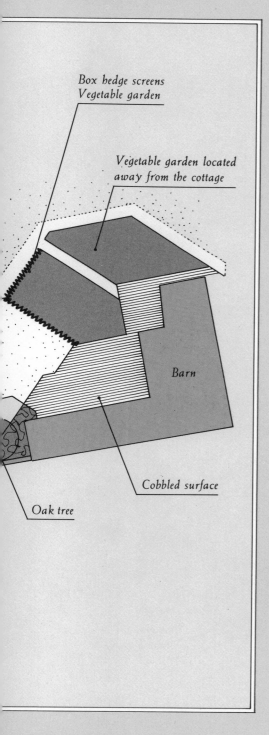

Box hedge screens Vegetable garden

Vegetable garden located away from the cottage

Barn

Cobbled surface

Oak tree

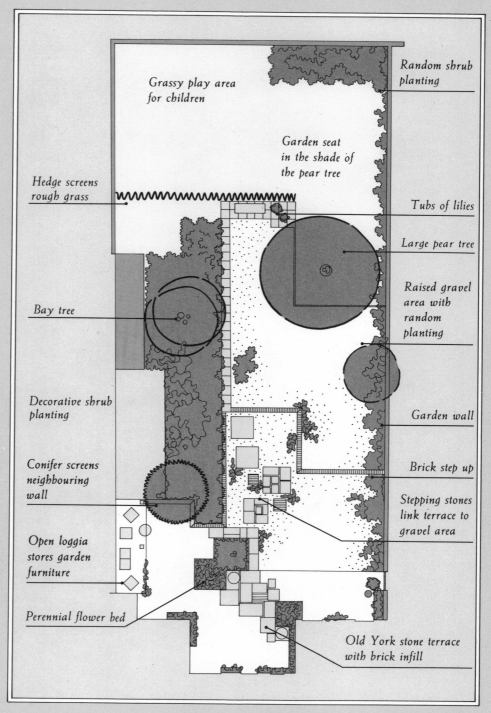

Grassy play area for children

Random shrub planting

Garden seat in the shade of the pear tree

Hedge screens rough grass

Tubs of lilies

Large pear tree

Bay tree

Raised gravel area with random planting

Decorative shrub planting

Garden wall

Conifer screens neighbouring wall

Brick step up

Stepping stones link terrace to gravel area

Open loggia stores garden furniture

Perennial flower bed

Old York stone terrace with brick infill

PRACTICAL AND NATURAL STYLE

The owners of this garden wanted a practical garden style involving little fuss and maintenance. So a soft and slightly wild approach was adopted, which works well in such a garden of less than 2.5 hectares (an acre).

A brick terrace has been built near the house, which is brightened with tubs of flowers. This leads on to a mown lawn and beyond this the view is directed towards some existing old fruit trees and bold swathes of rough grass planted with spring bulbs. A grassy mound edged with evergreens adds further interest. At the side of the house is a play area, with low-maintenance shrub planting at the front for year-round decoration.

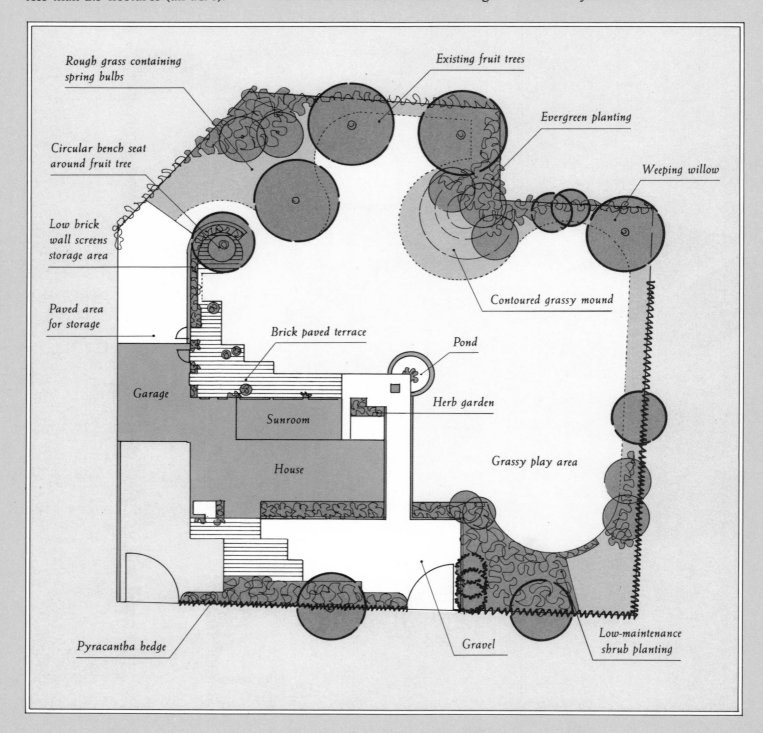

Rough grass containing spring bulbs

Existing fruit trees

Evergreen planting

Circular bench seat around fruit tree

Weeping willow

Low brick wall screens storage area

Contoured grassy mound

Paved area for storage

Brick paved terrace

Pond

Garage

Herb garden

Sunroom

Grassy play area

House

Pyracantha hedge

Gravel

Low-maintenance shrub planting

UTILIZING THE AVAILABLE SPACE

This house has a large area of land but only a small portion of it was used as a garden. This was behind the house, raised about 1.5m (4 ft) above ground level. It was a walled garden surrounded by tall neighbouring trees, which made it claustrophobic. The land to the south of the house was used as a random car parking area, restricting the view of a delightful barn.

The garden has now been extended. A terrace overlooks a new lawn and commands a view of the barn. A new rear entrance has been built and cars are restricted to this end of the yard. The walled garden is now a place for shrub roses and species bulbs growing in long grass.

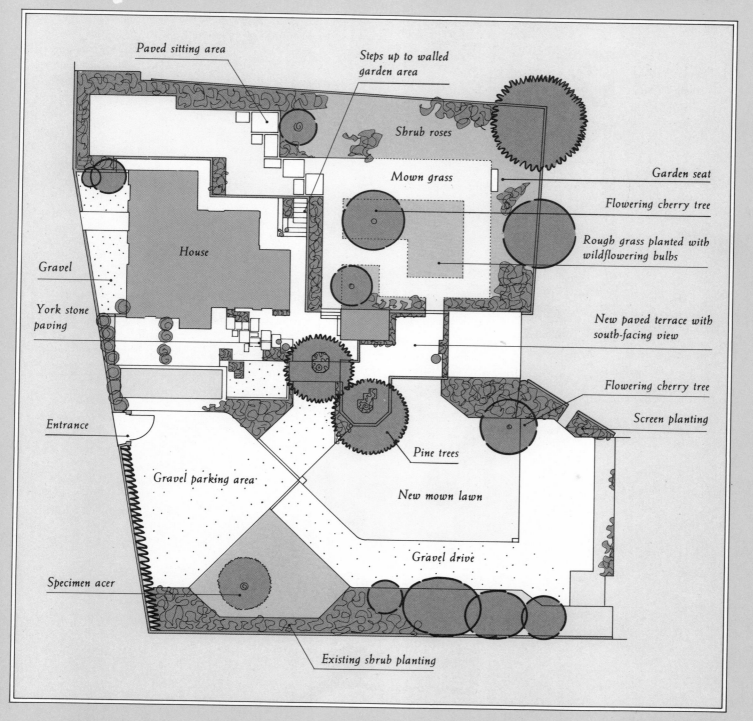

Paved sitting area

Steps up to walled garden area

Shrub roses

Mown grass

Garden seat

Flowering cherry tree

Rough grass planted with wildflowering bulbs

House

Gravel

York stone paving

New paved terrace with south-facing view

Flowering cherry tree

Screen planting

Entrance

Pine trees

Gravel parking area

New mown lawn

Gravel drive

Specimen acer

Existing shrub planting

OPENING UP A VIEW

This manor house has a large garden that was very formal and structured. The aim was to soften the design of the garden to make it more in tune with the surrounding countryside. The approach to the manor house has been left formal: a gravelled forecourt planted with plane trees. At the rear, a new L-shaped ha-ha allows an unrestricted view from the house out on to parkland. Elements of rougher grass have been introduced to frame the house and to help screen a swimming pool area at the side of the garden. The detailing round the house is now bolder and simpler, with wide stone terraces and rich shrub planting.

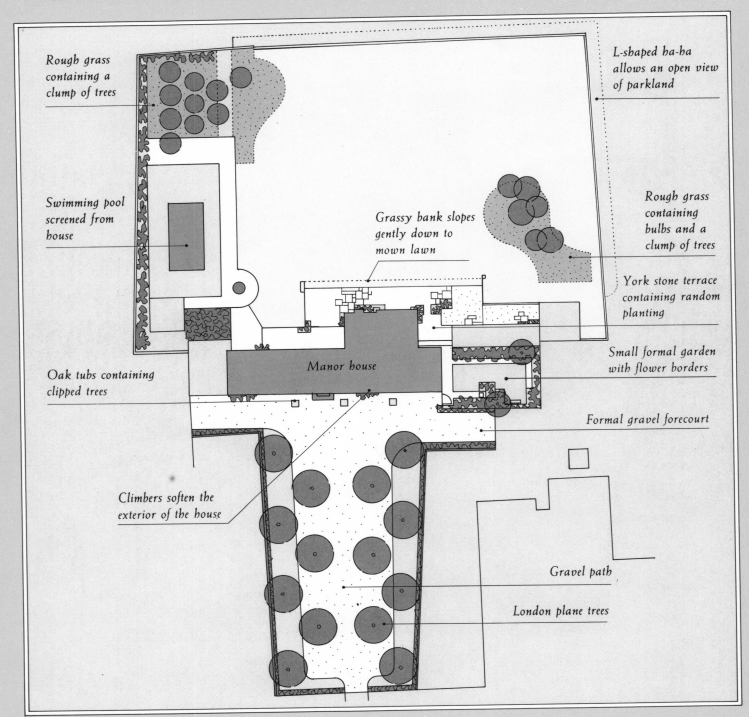

Rough grass containing a clump of trees

L-shaped ha-ha allows an open view of parkland

Swimming pool screened from house

Rough grass containing bulbs and a clump of trees

Grassy bank slopes gently down to mown lawn

York stone terrace containing random planting

Manor house

Small formal garden with flower borders

Oak tubs containing clipped trees

Formal gravel forecourt

Climbers soften the exterior of the house

Gravel path

London plane trees

RE-ORIENTATING A GARDEN

This house has a fine view south over cultivated fields. However, between the house and the fields was a fence and an ugly gravel car-turn, so the view could not be easily appreciated. It was decided to re-orientate the garden. So a more practical gravel forecourt has been created at the rear of the house and the original car-turn made into a lawn. Removing the boundary fence to the field now allows an open view from the house, which can be enjoyed from a new brick terrace built to overlook the fields. A copse of silver birch trees replaces the original gravel drive. The edges of the lawn are softened with rough grass containing bulbs.

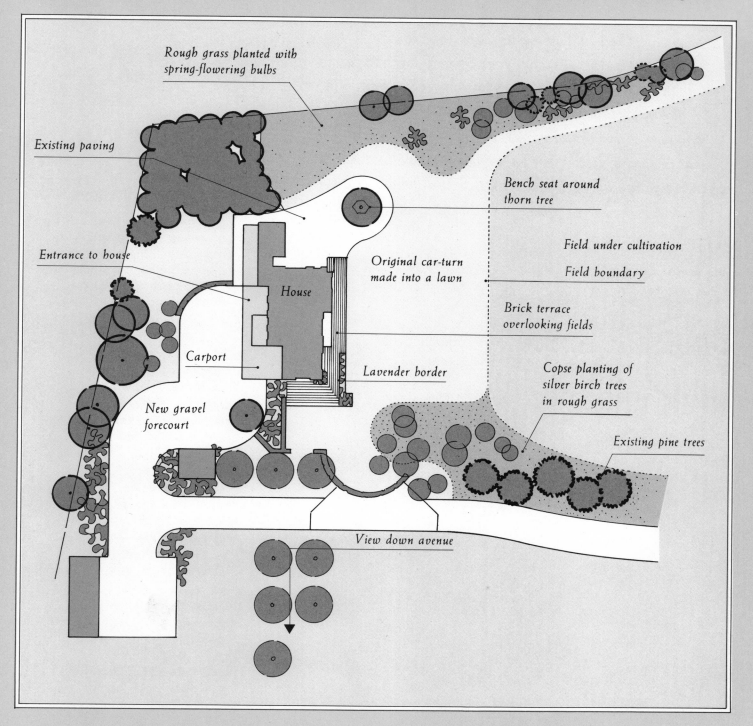

Rough grass planted with spring-flowering bulbs

Existing paving

Entrance to house

House

Carport

New gravel forecourt

Lavender border

Bench seat around thorn tree

Field under cultivation

Field boundary

Original car-turn made into a lawn

Brick terrace overlooking fields

Copse planting of silver birch trees in rough grass

Existing pine trees

View down avenue

PLANTS FOR A NATURAL LOOK

The following lists are a guide to finding plants that match your country location rather than clash with it. If you choose carefully, you will achieve a special harmony between the plants within your boundaries and those beyond. The plants are a mixture of native species, species that have become naturalized despite originating abroad, and plants, that although exotic, have a sufficiently "wild" look to suit a country style.

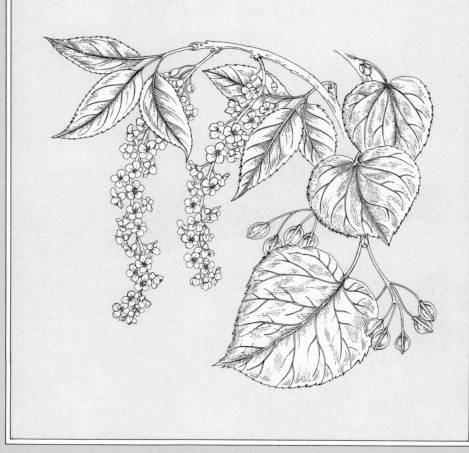

Juglans regia
Walnut

NATIVE TREES

Acer campestre Field maple
Acer platanoides Norway maple
Acer pseudoplatinus Sycamore
Aesculus hippocastanum Horse chestnut
Alnus cordata Italian alder
Alnus glutinosa Common alder
Alnus incana Grey alder
Betula pendula Silver birch
Betula pubescens Downy birch
Carpinus betula Hornbeam
Castanea sativa Sweet chestnut
Corylus avellana Hazel
Crataegus monogyna Hawthorn
Fagus sylvatica Beech
Fraxinus excelsior Ash
Ilex aquifolium Holly
Juglens regia Walnut
Malus sylvestris Wild crab apple
Pinus sylvestris Scots pine
Populus candicans 'Aurora' Golden variegated poplar
Populus canescens Grey poplar
Populus nigra italica Lombardy poplar
Populus tremula Aspen
Prunus avium Wild cherry
Prunus padus Bird cherry
Pyrus communis Common pear

Pyrus pyraster Wild pear
Quercus cernis Turkey oak
Quercus petraea Sessile oak
Quercus robur Common oak
Quercus rubra Red oak
Salix alba White willow
Salix alba 'Britzensis' Red willow
Salix alba 'Caerulea' Cricket bat willow
Salix caprea Goat willow
Salix cinerea Grey willow
Salix daphnoides Violet willow
Salix fragilis Crack willow
Salix pentandra Bay willow
Salix viminalis Osier
Salix vitellina Golden willow
Sorbus aria Whitebeam
Sorbus aucuparia Mountain ash
Sorbus intermedia Swedish whitebeam
Sorbus torminalis Wild service tree
Taxus baccata Yew
Taxus baccata 'Fastigiata' Irish yew
Tilia cordata Small-leaved lime
Tilia platyphyllos Broad-leaved lime
Ulmus glabra Wych elm
Ulmus procera English elm
Viburnum lantana Wayfaring tree

NATIVE SHRUBS

Lonicera periclymenum
Honeysuckle

Buxus sempervirens Box
Calluna vulgaris Heather/ling
Clematis vitalba Traveller's joy
Cornus alba Red-twigged dogwood
Cornus sanguinea Common dogwood
Corylus avellana Hazel
Crataegus laevigata Hawthorn
Crataegus monogyna Hawthorn
Cytisus scoparius Broom
Daphne laureola Spurge laurel
Erica cinerea Bell heather
Erica tetralix Cross-leaved heath
Euonymus europaeus Spindle tree
Frangula alnus Buckthorn
Hippophae rhamnoides Sea buckthorn
Hypericum androsaemum Tutsan
Juniperus communis Juniper
Ligustrum vulgare Wild privet
Lonicera periclymenum Honeysuckle
Myrica gale Bog myrtle
Prunus spinosa Wild blackthorn
Rhamnus cathartica Common buckthorn
Rhamnus frangula Alder buckthorn
Rosa arvensis Field rose
Rosa canina Dog rose
Rubus fruticosus Bramble
Ruscus asculeatus Butcher's broom
Salix cinerea Grey willow
Salix purpurea Purple willow
Salix viminalis Osier
Sambucus nigra Elder
Symphoricarpus albus Snowberry
Ulex europaeus Gorse
Vaccinium myrtillus Bilberry/Blackberry
Viburnum opulus Guelder rose

SHRUB ROSES FOR MASS PLANTING

Rosa 'Dunwich Rose'
Rosa nitida
Rosa 'Nozomi'
Rosa 'Paulii'
Rosa 'Red Blanket'
Rosa 'Rosa Cushion'
Rosa rugosa 'Frau Dagmar Hartopp'
Rosa rugosa 'Max Graf'
Rosa rugosa 'Smarty'
Rosa rugosa 'Swany'

Rosa rugosa
'Frau Dagmar Hartopp'

BAMBOOS AND GRASSES

BAMBOOS

Arundinaria fagamowskii
Arundinaria fastuosa
Arundinaria murielae
Arundinaria nitida
Arundinaria palmata
Arundinaria variegata
Arundinaria viridistriata
Phyllostachys aurea Golden bamboo
Phyllostachys flexuosa
Phyllostachys nigra Black bamboo
Phyllostachys nigra henonis
Phyllostachys viridi-glaucescens

GRASSES

Agrostis stolonifera Bent-creeping cloud grass
Agrostis tenuis Cloud grass
Alopecurus pratensis aureus Golden foxtail
Arundo donax Giant reed
Avena candida Oat grass
Bouteloua gracilis Mosquito grass
Brachypodium pinnatum Chalk false broom
Brachypodium sylvaticum Wood false broom
Briza media Quaking grass
Calamagrostis × *acutiflorus*

Briza media
Quaking grass

Carex morrowii variegata
Carex pendula
Carex riparia variegata
Cortaderia fulvida Pampas grass
Cortaderia pulmila
Cortaderia rendatlevi
Cortaderia richardii Toe-toe
Cortaderia richardii 'Sunningdale Silver'
Cortaderia selloana monstrosa
Cynosurus cristatus Dog's tail
Cyperus vegetus
Deschampsia caespitosa Tufted hair-grass
Deschampsia flexnosa Hair-grass
Elymus arenarius Lyme grass
Eriophorum angustifolium Cottongrass
Festuca amethystina Fescue grass
Festuca arundinacea Tall fescue
Festuca glacialis Fescue grass
Festuca ovina 'Glauca' Sheep's fescue
Festuca punctola Fescue grass
Festuca rubra Chewing fescue
Festuca tenuifolia Fine-leaved sheep's fescue
Glyceria aquatica variegata Sweet-grass
Glyceria fluitans Floating sweet-grass

Glyceria maxima 'Variegata' Reed small-grass
Glyceria plicata Plicate sweet-grass
Hakonechloa macra 'Albo-aurea'
Helictotrichon sempervirens
Holcus mollis 'Variegatus'
Hordeum murinum Meadow barley
Koeleria spp. Hair-grass
Lolium perenne Perennial rye-grass
Melica uniflora Wood melick
Milium effusum Wood millet
Milium effusum aureum Golden wood millet
Miscanthus sacchariflorus
Miscanthus sinensis 'Gracillimus'
Miscanthus sinensis 'Silver Feather'
Miscanthus sinensis variegata
Miscanthus sinensis 'Zebrinus'
Molinia altissima
Molinia coerulea 'Variegata' Purple moor-grass
Pennisetum orientale
Pennisetum setaceum Fountain grass
Phalaris arundinacea 'Picta' Gardener's garters
Phleum pratense Timothy
Poa pratensis Smooth meadow-grass
Poa trivialia Rough meadow-grass
Scirpus tabernaemontani Grey club-rush
Spartina pectinata 'Aureo-marginata' Cord-grass
Stipa arundinacea Feather grass
Stipa calamagrostis
Stipa gigantea
Uniola latifolia

WILD FLOWERS

WOODLAND
Digitalis purpurea Foxglove
Hypericum hirsutum Hairy St John's wort
Lychnis flos-cuculi Ragged Robin
Myosotis arvensis Field forget-me-not
Silene dioica Red campion
Stachys sylvatica Hedge woundwort

HEDGEROW
Achillea millefolium Yarrow
Campanula rotundifolia Harebell

Chrysanthemum leucanthemum Oxeye daisy
Digitalis purpurea Foxglove
Hypericum perforatum Perforate St John's wort
Myosotis arvensis Field forget-me-not
Petroselinum sativum Sheep's parsley
Prunella vulgaris Selfheal
Silene dioica Red campion
Stachys sylvatica Hedge woundwort

COASTAL
Achillea millefolium Yarrow
Anthyllis vulneraria Kidney vetch
Campanula rotundifolia Harebell
Galium verum Lady's bedstraw
Lotus corniculatus Common bird's foot trefoil
Myosotis arvensis Field forget-me-not

ACID SOIL
Campanula rotundifolia Harebell
Cichorium intybus Chicory
Digitalis purpurea Foxglove
Dipsacus fullonum Teasel
Hypericum perforatum Perforate St John's wort
Hypericum pulchrum Slender St John's wort

Myosotis arvenis
Field forget-me-not

LIME SOIL

Achillea millefolium Yarrow
Anthyllis vulneraria Kidney vetch
Campanula rotundifolia Harebell
Chrysanthemum leucanthemum
  Oxeye daisy
Cichorium intybus Chicory
Galium verum Lady's bedstraw
Hypericum perforatum Perforate St
  John's wort
Lotus corniculatus Common bird's
  foot trefoil
Medicago lupulina Black medick
Plantago lanceolata Ribwort plantain
Prunella vulgaris Selfheal
Sanguisorba minor Salad burnet

CLAY SOIL

Achillea millefolium Yarrow
Anthyllis vulneraria Kidney vetch
Chrysanthemum leucanthemum
  Oxeye daisy
Galium verum Lady's bedstraw
Lotus corniculatus Common bird's
  foot trefoil
Medicago lupulina Black medick
Plantago lanceolata Ribwort plantain
Prunella vulgaris Selfheal
Silene alba White campion

LOAM

Chrysanthemum leucanthemum
  Oxeye daisy
Galium verum Lady's bedstraw
Lotus corniculatus Common bird's
  foot trefoil
Lychnis flos-cuculi Ragged Robin
Medicago lupulina Black medick
Petroselinum sativum Sheep's parsley
Plantago lanceolata Ribwort plantain
Prunella vulgaris Selfheal
Sanguisorba minor Salad burnet

GROUNDCOVER PLANTS

DRY SHADED AREAS

Acanthus longifolius
Acanthus mollis Bear's breeches
Alchemilla mollis Lady's mantle
Anaphalis triplinervis
Artemisia spp. Wormwood

Viola canina
Dog violet

Berberis spp. Barberry
Brunnera macrophylla
Cornus canadensis Dogwood
Epimedium perralderianum
  Barrenwort
Euphorbia spp. Spurge
Festuca glauca Fescue grass
Geranium spp. Cranesbill
Hedera spp. Ivy
Heuchera spp.
Hypericum spp. St John's wort
Iris foetidissima Gladwyn iris
Lamium spp. Dead-nettle
Lavandula spp. Lavender
Liriope muscari
Mahonia aquifolium Oregon grape
Omphalodes cappadocica
Pachysandra terminalis
Polygonatum spp. Solomon's seal
Polygonum spp. Knotweed
Prunus zabeliana
Pulmonaria spp. Lungwort
Sarcococca humilis Sweet box
Stachys spp. Woundwort
Symphoricarpus spp. Snowberry
Tiarella cordifolia Foam flower
Vinca minor Lesser periwinkle
Waldsteinia spp.

MOIST SHADED AREAS

Ajuga spp. Bugle
Alchemilla spp. Lady's mantle
Astrantia spp. Masterwort

Bergenia spp.
Caltha spp. Kingcup
Cornus canadensis Dogwood
Epimedium spp. Barrenwort
Hosta spp. Plantain lily
Leucothoe fontanesiana
Lysimachia spp. Loosestrife
Polygonatum spp. Solomon's seal
Polygonum spp. Knotgrass
Primula spp. Primrose
Pulmonaria spp. Lungwort
Salix spp. Willow

WILDLIFE FOOD PLANTS

TREES AND SHRUBS

Amelanchier lamarckii
Arbutus spp.
Arctostaphylos uva-ursi Bearberry
Aucuba japonica
Berberis spp. Berberry
Buddleia spp. Butterfly bush
Callicarpa 'Profusion'
Chaenomeles spp. Flowering quince
Clerodendrum trichotomum
Colutea arborescens Bladder senna
Cornus spp. Dogwood
Corylus avellana Hazel
Corylus maxima 'Purpurea' Filbert
Cotoneaster spp.
Crataegus monogyna Hawthorn
Daphne mezereum Mezereon
Decaisnea fargesii
Dorycnium spp.
Euonymus europaeus 'Intermedius'
  Spindle tree
Euonymus europaeus 'Red Cascade'
Euonymus sachalinensis
Euonymus yedoensis
Gaultheria procumbens
Hebe spp.
Hippophae rhamnoides Sea buckthorn
Hypericum androsaemum Tutsan
Hypericum forestii St John's wort
Hypericum indorum 'Elstead'
Ilex spp. Holly
Lonicera periclymenum Honeysuckle
Mahonia spp.
Malus spp. Apple
Nandina domestica Sacred bamboo

Papaver rhoeas
Poppy

Osmanthus decora
Pernettya mucronata 'Bell's Seedling'
  Prickly heath
Poncirus trifoliata Hardy orange
Populus nigra Black poplar
Prunus spp. Cherry
Pyracantha spp. Firethorn
Rhamnus frangula Buckthorn
Rhus typhina Sumach
Ribes odoratum Buffalo currant
Rosa spp. Rose
Rubus spp. Bramble
Ruscus aculeatus Butcher's broom
Salix spp. Willow
Sambucus spp. Elder
Skimmia spp.
Sorbus spp. Rowan
Staphylea spp. Bladder nut
Stranvaesia spp.
Symphoricarpos spp. Snowberry
Syringa spp. Lilac
Taxus spp. Yew
Vaccinium myrtillus Bilberry
Viburnum davidii
Viburnum lantana Wayfaring tree
Viburnum opulus Guelder rose
Vitis spp. Vine

GARDEN FLOWERS
Antirrhinum spp. Snapdragon
Aster spp. Michaelmas daisy
Cosmos spp.
Helianthus spp. Sunflower
Scabiosa spp. Scabious

WILD PLANTS
Carlina vulgaris Thistle
Centaurea nigra Hardheads
Dipsacus fullonum Teasel
Papaver rhoeas Poppy
Senecio jacobaea Ragwort
Urtica dioica Nettle

FOOD PLANTS FOR BUTTERFLIES

Achillea millefolium Yarrow
Alliaria petiolata Garlic mustard
Alyssum spp. Madwort
Anthyllis vulneraria Kidney vetch
Armeria maritima Thrift
Aster spp. Michaelmas daisy
Buddleia davidii Butterfly bush
Cardamine pratensis Cuckooflower
Centaurea cyanus Cornflower
Cirsium vulgare Spear thistle
Cytisus scoparius Broom
Dactylis glomerata Cock's foot
Dianthus spp. Pink
Erigeron acer Blue fleabane
Erodium cicutarium Common
  stork's bill
Eupatorium cannabinum Hemp
  agrimony
Fragaria vesca Wild strawberry
Helenium spp. Sneezeweed

Trifolium repens
White clover

Helianthemum nummularium
  Common rock rose
Heliotropium spp. Heliotrope
Hesperis matronalis Dame's violet
Hippocrepis comosa Horseshoe vetch
Hyssopus officinalis Hyssop
Iberis umbellata Candytuft
Lavandula angustifolia Lavender
Lippia citriodora Verbena
Lonicera periclymenum Honeysuckle
Lotus corniculatus Common bird's
  foot trefoil
Lunaria annua Honesty
Lychnis flos-cuculi Ragged Robin
Lythrum salicaria Purple loosestrife
Myosotis arvensis Field forget-me-not
Nepeta cataria Cat mint
Ononis repens Common restharrow
Origanum spp. Marjoram
Plantago lanceolata Ribwort plantain
Poa trivialis Rough meadow-grass
Primula spp. Polyanthus
Prunus spinosa Blackthorn
Reseda odorata Mignonette
Rhamnus frangula Buckthorn
Rubus fruticosus Bramble
Rumex acetosa Common sorrel
Salix caprea Goat willow
Scabiosa spp. Scabious
Sedum spectabile Ice plant
Solidago virgaurea Goldenrod
Succisa pratensis Devil's-bit scabious
Syringa spp. Lilac
Thymus spp. Thyme
Trifolium repens White clover
Tussilago farfara Colt's foot
Ulex europaeus Gorse
Urtica dioica Common nettle
Valeriana spp. Valerian
Viola spp. Violet

FOOD PLANTS FOR BEES

TREES
Acer spp. Maple
Aesculus spp. Horse chestnut
Ailanthus altissima Tree-of-Heaven
Alnus glutinosa Alder
Alnus incana and forms Alder
Caragana arborescens
Castanea sativa Spanish chestnut

Malus sp.
Apple

Catalpa bignonioides
Cotoneaster frigidus
Crataegus prunifolia Thorn
Fagus spp. Beech
Fraxinus excelsior Common ash
Koelreuteria spp.
Liquidambar styraciflua Sweet gum
Liriodendron tulipifera Tulip tree
Malus spp. Apple
Mespilus germanica Medlar
Populus nigra Black poplar
Populus tremula Aspen
Prunus spp.
Quercus spp. Oak
Robinia pseudoacacia False acacia
Salix aria and forms Willow
Salix aucuparia and forms Willow
Tilia × *euchlora* Lime tree

SHRUBS

Aesculus parviflora Dwarf buckeye
Amelanchier ovalis
Arbutus spp.
Berberis spp. Barberry
Buddleia globosa
Buxus spp. Box
Ceanothus spp.
Cercis siliquastrum Judas tree
Chaenomeles japonica Japanese quince
Colutea spp. Bladder senna
Cornus sanguinea Dogwood
Cotoneaster spp.

Cytisus spp. Broom
Daphne mezereum Mezereon
Elaeagnus spp.
Escallonia spp.
Helianthemum nummularium Rock rose
Hypericum androsaemum Tutsan
Hypericum forrestii
Ilex spp. Holly
Laurus nobilis Sweet bay
Olearia spp. Daisy bush
Prunus laurocerasus and forms
Pyracantha spp. Firethorn
Rhamnus frangula Alder buckthorn
Rhus spp. Sumach
Ribes sanguineum Flowering currant
Ribes speciosum Fuchsia-flowered
    gooseberry
Salix caprea Goat willow
Salix repens argentea Creeping willow
Skimmia spp.
Spiraea spp.
Staphylea spp. Bladder nut
Stephanandra spp.
Stranvaesia spp.
Symphoricarpus spp.
Syringa spp. Lilac
Tamarix 'Pink Cascade' Tamarisk
Thymus spp. Thyme
Ulex europaeus Gorse
Viburnum opulus Guelder rose
Viburnum tinus
Weigela spp.

Ribes sanguineum
Flowering currant

PERENNIALS

Aconitum napellus Monk's-hood
Allium schoenoprasum Chives
Alyssum saxatile
Anchusa officinalis Bugloss
Armeria maritima Thrift
Aster spp. Michaelmas daisy
Centaurea cyanus Cornflower
Centaurea nigra Hardheads
Centaurea scabiosa Greater knapweed
Cheiranthus spp. Wallflower
Colchicum spp.
Coreopsis spp.
Delphinium spp. Larkspur
Digitalis purpurea Foxglove
Dipsacus fullonum Teasel
Echinops spp. Globe thistle
Endymion non-scriptus Bluebell
Epilobium angustifolium Rosebay
    willowherb
Eryngium maritimum Sea holly
Geranium pratense Meadow
    cranesbill
Iberis umbellata Candytuft
Inula conyza Ploughman's spikenard
Knautia arvensis Field scabious
Limonium spp. Sea lavender
Lobelia spp.
Lupinus spp. Lupin
Lythrum salicaria Purple loosestrife
Malva moschata Musk mallow
Malva sylvestris Common mallow
Melissa spp. Balm
Mertensia virginica Virginia cowslip
Narcissus spp.
Nepeta cataria Cat mint
Potentilla spp. Cinquefoil
Pulmonaria officinalis Lungwort
Ranunculus acris Meadow buttercup
Ranunculus ficaria Lesser celandine
Salvia officinalis Common sage
Salvia pratensis Meadow clary
Scabiosa columbaria Small scabious
Sedum spectabile Ice plant
Senecio spp.
Solidago virgaurea Goldenrod
Succisa pratensis Devil's-bit scabious
Tropaeolum spp. Nasturtium
Tussilago farfara Colt's foot
Verbascum nigrum Dark mullein
Veronica spp. Speedwell
Viola odorata Sweet violet

RABBIT-RESISTANT PLANTS

Polygonatum odoratum
Solomon's seal

TREES AND SHRUBS
Arbutus spp.
Aucuba spp.
Berberis spp. Barberry
Betula spp. Birch
Buddleia spp. Butterfly bush
Buxus spp. Box
Ceanothus spp.
Cornus sanguinea Dogwood
Cotoneaster spp. (not *C. simonsii*)
Daphne mezereum Mezereon
Deutzia scabra
Elaeagnus pungens 'Maculata'
Gaultheria spp.
Hippophae rhamnoides Sea buckthorn
Hydrangea spp.
Ilex spp. Holly
Kalmia latifolia Calico bush
Laburnum spp.
Lonicera spp. Honeysuckle
Olearia spp. Daisy bush
Paeonia (Moutan spp.) Tree paeony
Pernettya mucronata Prickly heath
Philadelphus spp. Mock orange
Pinus nigra Austrian pine
Rhus spp. Sumach
Ribes spp. Currant
Rosa (spiny species) Rose
Rosmarinus spp. Rosemary

Ruscus aculeatus Butcher's broom
Sambucus spp. Elder
Skimmia japonica
Spiraea spp.
Syringa spp. Lilac
Taxus spp. Yew
Ulex spp. Gorse
Viburnum lantana Wayfaring tree
Viburnum opulus Guelder rose

PERENNIALS
Anemone spp. Windflower
Aquilegia spp. Columbine
Astilbe spp. False goatsbeard
Epimedium spp. Barrenwort
Euphorbia spp. Spurge
Geranium spp. Cranesbill
Helleborus spp. Hellebore
Hemerocallis spp. Day lily
Kniphofia spp. Torch lily
Lupinus spp. Lupin
Polygonatum spp. Solomon's seal
Salvia × *superba*
Sedum spectabile Ice plant

FERNS FOR NATURALIZING

Blechnum spicant
Hard fern

Asplenium scolopendrium Spleenwort
Blechnum spicant Hard fern
Dryopteris austriaca Broad buckler fern

Dryopteris filix-mas Male fern
Phyllitis scolopendrium Hart's tongue fern
Polypodium vulgare Common polypody
Polystichum acutilobum
Polystichum setiferum

BULBS FOR NATURALIZING

Colchicum speciosum
'Album'

Allium spp.
Anemone apennina Windflower
Anemone blanda Windflower
Anemone nemorosa Windflower
Chionodoxa spp. Glory of the snow
Colchicum kotchyanus
Colchicum speciosum
Erythronium dens-canis
Narcissus obvallaris 'Beryl'
Narcissus obvallaris 'Golden Cycle'
Narcissus obvallaris 'Larkelly'
Narcissus obvallaris 'March Sunshine'
Narcissus obvallaris 'Piper's Barn'
Narcissus obvallaris 'Rockery White'
Narcissus pseudonarcissus Wild daffodil
Narcissus triandrus
Narcissus triandrus 'Rippling Waters'
Narcissus triandrus 'Thalia'
Scilla bifolia
Scilla lilio-hyacinthina
Scilla sibirica Siberian squill

PLANTS FOR COUNTRY MOODS AND PLEASURES

*The following plant lists reflect
some of the seasonal pleasures of the country garden,
encompassing colours, shapes and textures. You will find
that most of the plants included will fit into mixed
planting schemes admirably, depending on your taste, but
if you want to grow large quantities of specific plants
to fulfil the requirements of a hobby or other employment,
consider growing them separately in bold masses.*

COTTAGE GARDEN

Digitalis purpurea
Foxglove

Achillea spp. Yarrow
Althaea spp. Hollyhock
Alyssum spp. Madwort
Amelanchier ovalis
Anchusa spp. Alkanet
Antirrhinum spp. Snapdragon
Aster spp. Michaelmas daisy
Berberis spp. Barberry
Buddleia davidii Butterfly bush
Cardamine pratensis Cuckoo-flower
Centaurea cyanus Cornflower
Centaurea nigra Hardheads
Chaenomeles japonica Japanese quince
Cheiranthus spp. Wallflower
Cirsium vulgare Spear thistle
Cistus spp. Rock rose
Colchicum spp.
Colutea spp. Bladder senna
Cornus spp. Dogwood
Cosmos spp.
Cotoneaster spp.
Cynosurus cristatus Crested dog's tail
Dactylis glomerata Cock's foot
Delphinium spp. Larkspur
Dianthus spp. Pink
Digitalis purpurea Foxglove
Dipsacus fullonum Teasel
Echinops spp. Globe thistle

Endymion non-scriptus Bluebell
Fragaria vesca Wild strawberry
Godetia spp.
Hedera spp. Ivy
Helianthemum nummularium Rock rose
Helianthus annuus Sunflower
Hippocrepis comosa Horseshoe vetch
Humulus lupulus Wild hop
Hyssopus officinalis Hyssop
Iberis spp. Candytuft
Jasminum spp. Jasmine
Lathyrus latifolius Everlasting pea
Lavandula spp. Lavender
Lippia citriodora Verbena
Lobelia spp.
Lonicera periclymenum Honeysuckle
Lotus corniculatus Common bird's
    foot trefoil
Lunaria annua Honesty
Lupinus spp. Lupin
Lychnis flos-cuculi Ragged Robin
Lythrum salicaria Purple loosestrife
Malva sylvestris Common mallow
Matthiola bicornis Night-scented stock
Medicago sativa Lucerne
Myosotis arvensis Field forget-me-not
Narcissus spp.
Nepeta cataria Cat mint
Nicotiana spp. Tobacco plant
Oenothera biennis Evening primrose
Ononis repens Common restharrow
Petunia spp.
Phlox spp.
Plantago lanceolata Ribwort plantain
Primula veris Polyanthus
Pulmonaria officinalis Lungwort
Ranunculus ficaria Lesser celandine
Reseda lutea Mignonette
Rosa spp. (scented shrub roses) Rose
Salvia spp. Sage
Saponaria officinalis Soapwort
Scabiosa spp. Scabious
Sedum spectabile Ice plant
Solidago virgaurea Goldenrod
Thymus spp. Thyme
Trifolium repens White clover
Tropaeolum spp. Nasturtium
Valeriana spp. Valerian
Verbascum nigrum Dark mullein
Veronica spp. Speedwell
Viburnum opulus Guelder rose
Viola odorata Sweet violet

COLOURFUL PERENNIALS

Helleborus niger
Christmas rose

YELLOW
Achillea 'Moonshine' Yarrow
Anthemis tinctoria 'Mrs E C Buxton'
Digitalis grandiflora Foxglove
Euphorbia wulfenii Spurge
Ligularia clivorum 'Desdemona'
Lysimachia punctata Loosestrife
Paeonia mlokosewitschii
Sisyrinchium striatum
Verbascum olympicum Mullein

BLUE
Agapanthus Headbourne hybrid
    African lily
Anchusa azurea
Aster frikartii Michaelmas daisy
Brunnera macrophylla
Campanula persicifolia Bellflower
Echinops ritro Globe thistle
Geranium 'Johnson's Blue' Cranesbill
Iris pallida variegata
Omphalodes cappadocica
Salvia × *superba*
Veronica spp. Speedwell

RED
Bergenia 'Evening Glow'
Helenium 'Moerheim Beauty'
Hemerocallis spp. Day lily
Iris 'Solid Mahogany'

Papaver spp. Poppy
Phlox 'Brigadier'
Sedum 'Ruby Glow'

WHITE
Achillea ptarmica 'The Pearl' Yarrow
Agapanthus campanulatus African lily
Bergenia 'Silver Light'
Chrysanthemum maximum
Dianthus 'White Ladies'
Helleborus niger Christmas rose
Hosta plantaginea Plantain lily
Libertia formosa
Phlox 'White Admiral'
Polygonatum multiflorum

GREEN
Alchemilla mollis Lady's mantle
Euphorbia characias Spurge
Euphorbia robbiae Spurge
Galtonia viride
Helleborus corsicus
Zantedeschia aethiopica 'Green
    Goddess' Arum lily

HANDSOME FOLIAGE PLANTS

Acanthus spp. Bear's breeches
Acorus spp.
Alchemilla spp. Lady's mantle
Artemisia spp.

Hosta sp.
Plantain lily

Arum italicum 'Pictum' Italian arum
Astrantia 'Variegata' Masterwort
Ballota spp.
Bergenia spp.
Brunnera spp.
Carex spp. Blue grass
Crambe spp. Seakale
Cynara spp.
Daphne odora aureo-reticulata
Epimedium spp. Barrenwort
Euonymus spp. Spindle tree
Euphorbia spp. Spurge
Festuca spp. Fescue grass
Filipendula spp. Meadowsweet
Glaucium phoenicium Horned poppy
Gunnera spp.
Hedera spp. Ivy
Helleborus spp. Hellebore
Heuchera americana Alum root
Hosta spp. Plantain lily
Iris foetidissima Gladwyn iris
Kniphofia nothiae Torch lily
Lamium spp.
Libertia spp.
Ligularia spp.
Lonicera nitida 'Baggesen's Gold'
Lysichitum spp.
Lysimachia nummularia 'Aurea'
Melissa 'Aurea' Golden balm
Milium effusum aureum Bowles'
    golden grass millet
Onopordum spp.
Origanum vulgare aureum
Phormium tenax New Zealand flax
Physocarpus opulifolia lutens
Rheum palmatum Rhubarb
Rodgersia podophylla
Ruta graveolens and forms Rue
Salvia argentea Sage
Salvia officinalis and forms Sage
Saxifraga fortunei and forms
Scrophularia nodosa 'Variegata'
Senecio spp.
Sisyrinchium 'Variegatum'
Stipa spp. Feather grass
Tellima grandiflora
Thymus 'Golden Carpet' Thyme
Tovara spp.
Trachystemon spp.
Trifolium repens 'Purpurea'
Valeriana phu 'Aurea' Valerian
Verbascum olympicum Mullein

DECORATIVE SEEDHEADS

Cardoon and honesty

Acanthus spinosus Bear's breeches
Achillea filipendulina Yarrow
Agapanthus spp. African lily
Allium aflatunense
Aquilegia spp. Columbine
Armeria spp. Thrift
Artemisia purshiana
Asphodeline lutea Asphodel
Carex pendula Blue grass
Carlina acaulis 'Caulescens'
Cortaderia selloana Pampas grass
Cynara cardunculus Cardoon
Cyperus spp.
Dictamnus spp.
Eryngium spp.
Filipendula spp. Meadowsweet
Hosta spp. Plantain lily
Incarvillea spp.
Iris chrysographes
Iris foetidissima Gladwyn iris
Iris innominata
Iris sibirica
Lunaria rediviva Honesty
Lysimachia ephemerum Loosestrife
Morina spp. Whorl flower
Pennisetum orientale
Phlomis samia
Physalis franchettii Bladder herb
Pulsatilla vulgaris Pasque flower

Rhus cotinus Sumach
Stachys 'Cotton Boll' Woundwort
Stipa spp. Feather grass
Thalictrum aquilegifolium Meadow rue
Verbascum chaixii Nettle-leaved
    mullein

COLOURED STEMS

Acer palmatum 'Senkaki' Coral-bark
    maple
Arbutus andrachne
Cornus spp. Dogwood
Euonymus phellomanus
Kerria japonica Jew's mallow
Leucothoe fontanesiana 'Rainbow'
Leycesteria formosa
Perovskia × 'Blue Spire'
Poncirus trifoliata Hardy orange
Ribes speciosum
Rubus biflorus Wineberry
Rubus cockburnianus
Rubus thibetanus
Salix alba 'Chermesina' White willow
Salix atrocinerea
Salix elaeagnos
Salix fargesii
Salix triandra
Salix alba vitellina Golden willow
Spartium junceum Spanish broom
Stephanandra incisa 'Crispa'
Stephanandra tanakae

Salix alba 'Chermesina'
White willow cv.

AUTUMN INTEREST

Quercus rubra
Red oak

TREES
Acer spp. Maple
Aesculus hippocastanum Horse
  chestnut
Amelanchier lamarckii
Betula pendula Birch
Carpinus betulus Hornbeam
Crataegus lavalei Hawthorn
Fagus sylvatica Beech
Fraxinus excelsior 'Altena' Ash
Fraxinus oxycarpa 'Raywood'
Malus coronaria Apple
Populus alba White poplar
Prunus spp.
Quercus rubra Red oak
Sequoia spp. Californian redwood
Sorbus aucuparia Mountain ash

SHRUBS
Abelia spp.
Aronia spp.
Berberis spp. Barberry
Buddleia spp. Butterfly bush
Callicarpa spp.
Ceratostigma spp.
Cercidiphyllum spp.
Clethra spp.
Cornus spp. Dogwood
Corylopsis spp.

Cotinus spp.
Cotoneaster spp.
Deutzia spp.
Enkianthus spp.
Euonymus spp. Spindle tree
Fothergilla spp. American witch hazel
Hamamelis spp. Witch hazel
Hebe spp.
Hydrangea quercifolia
Kerria spp. Jew's mallow
Leucothoe spp.
Lindera spp.
Osmanthus spp.
Pachysandra spp.
Parrotia spp.
Parthenocissus spp.
Petrophytum spp.
Phlomis spp.
Pieris spp.
Potentilla spp. Cinquefoil
Punica spp.
Rhamnus spp. Buckthorn
Rhus spp. Sumach
Ribes spp.
Rosa rubrifolia Rose
Rosa rugosa Rose
Sambucus spp. Elder
Santolina spp. Cotton lavender
Senecio spp.
Stephanandra spp.
Teucrium spp. Germander
Vaccinium spp.
Viburnum spp.
Vitis spp. Vine

Sambucus sp.
Elder

WINTER FLOWERS

Galanthus nivalis
Snowdrop

Abeliophyllum spp.
Bergenia spp.
Camellia sasanqua
Chimonanthus praecox Winter sweet
Clematis balearica Virgin's bower
Colchicum spp. Crocus
Daphne mezereum Mezereon
Eranthis spp. Winter aconite
Erica carnea
Euphorbia spp. Spurge
Fatsia japonica Japanese aralia
Galanthus spp. Snowdrop
Garrya elliptica Silk tassel bush
Hamamelis spp. Witch hazel
Helleborus spp. Hellebore
Jasminium nudiflorum Winter jasmine
Lonicera fragrantissima Honeysuckle
Mahonia japonica
Osmanthus spp.
Pachysandra spp.
Parrotia spp.
Pulmonaria sacchakata
Rhododendron spp.
Sarcococca spp. Sweet box
Skimmia spp.
Stachyurus spp.
Viburnum bodnantense
Viburnum farreri
Viburnum tinus

DECORATIVE VEGETABLES

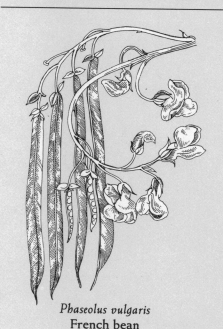

Phaseolus vulgaris
French bean

Abeliophyllum spp.
Allium cepa Onion (Welsh and tree)
Brassica oleracea capitata Cabbages (red, flowering or decorative)
Brassica oleracea italica Purple sprouting broccoli
Cichorium endivia Endive
Crambe maritima Chard
Cucurbita pepo Marrows, courgettes and squashes
Cynara cardunculus Cardoon
Cynara scolymus Globe artichoke
Zea mays Sweet corn

HERBS

Alkanna tinctoria Alkanet
Allium sativum Garlic
Allium schoenoprasum Chives
Althaea officinalis Marshmallow
Anethum graveolens Dill
Angelica archangelica Angelica
Anthemis nobilis Chamomile
Anthriscus cerefolium Chervil
Artimisia dracunculus Tarragon
Asperula odorata Woodruff
Borago officinalis Borage
Calendula officinalis Marigold

Carum carvi Caraway
Coriandrum sativum Coriander
Cuminum cyminum Cumin
Foeniculum vulgare Fennel
Galega officinalis Goat's rue
Helianthus annuus Sunflower
Helichrysum angustifolium Curry plant
Hyssopus officinalis Hyssop
Laurus nobilis Bay
Lavandula angustifolia Lavender
Levisticum officinalis Lovage
Lippia citriodora Verbena
Melissa officinalis Lemon balm
Mentha piperita Peppermint
Mentha rotundifolia Apple mint
Mentha viride Spearmint
Monarda didyma Bergamot
Myrrhis odorata Sweet cicely
Ocimum basilicum Basil
Ocimum minimum Bush basil
Origanum marjorana Sweet marjoram
Origanum onites Pot marjoram
Origanum vulgare and forms Wild marjoram
Petroselinum crispum Parsley
Polygonum bistorta Boneset
Portulaca deracea Purslane
Poterium sanguisorba Burnet
Rosmarinus lavandulaceus
Rosmarinus officinalis Rosemary
Rumex acetosa Sorrel
Ruta graveolens Rue
Salvia officinalis Sage

Humulus lupulus
Wild hop

Satureia hortensis Summer savory
Satureia montana Winter savory
Symphytum officinale Comfrey
Tanacetum vulgare Tansy
Thymus citriodorus Lemon thyme
Thymus vulgaris Common thyme
Tropaeolum majus Nasturtium

FRUIT AND NUTS

Blackberries and
cooking apple

Castanea sativa Spanish chestnut
Chaenomeles spp.
Corylus maxima Filbert
Ficus spp. Fig (Brown turkey)
Fragaria spp. Strawberry
Juglans regia Walnut
Malus spp. Apple
Malus spp. Crab apple
Mespilus germanica Medlar
Morus nigra Mulberry
Prunus armeniaca Apricot
Prunus domestica and forms Plum
Prunus persica and forms Peach
Prunus spp. Cherry
Prunus spp. Damson
Pyrus spp. Pear
Ribes spp. Currant (red, white and black)
Ribes uva-crispa Gooseberry
Rubus spp. Blackberry
Rubus idaeus Raspberry
Rubus idaeus × fruticosus Tay berry
Vitis spp. Vine

FLOWERS FOR DRYING

Sedum album
stonecrop

Acanthus spinosus Bear's breeches
Achillea filipendulina Yarrow
Acrolinium spp.
Allium aflatunense
Althaea spp. Hollyhock
Aquilegia spp. Columbine
Astrantia spp. Masterwort
Bellis spp. Daisy
Calendula spp. Marigold
Cheiranthus spp. Wallflower
Clarkia spp.
Clematis vitalba Traveller's joy
Convollaria spp. Lily-of-the-valley
Cynara scolymus Globe artichoke
Cytisus spp. Broom
Delphinium consolida Larkspur
Dianthus barbatus Sweet william
Dianthus carophyllus Carnation
Echinops ritro Globe thistle
Endymion non-scriptus Bluebell
Erica cinerea Heather
Eryngium maritimum Sea holly
Forsythia spp. Golden bells
Glixia spp.
Helichrysum angustifolium Everlastings
Humulus lupulus Hop
Hyacinthus spp. Hyacinth
Laburnum spp.

Lathyrus odoratus Sweet pea
Lavatera spp. Mallow
Lavandula spica Lavender
Limonium caspia Sea lavender
Lupinus spp. Lupin
Matthiola spp. Stock
Mollucella laevis Bells-of-Ireland
Nigella damascena Love-in-a-mist
Papaver Poppy
Primula veris Polyanthus
Rhodanthe spp.
Rosa spp. Rose
Santolina spp. Cotton lavender
Saxifraga umbrosa London pride
Sedum spp. Stonecrop
Senecio greyii
Solidago canadensis Goldenrod
Spiraea spp.
Stachys lanata Lamb's ears
Syringa spp. Lilac
Viola wittrockiana Pansy
Xeranthemum spp. Immortelle
Zinnia spp. Youth-and-old-age

HEDGING PLANTS

FORMAL
Acer campestre Field maple
Buxus sempervirens (evergreen) Box
Carpinus betulus Hornbeam
Corylus avellana Hazel
Crataegus spp. Hawthorn
Elaeagnus spp. (evergreen)
Escallonia spp. (evergreen) Chilean
    gum box
Euonymus japonicus Evergreen
    spindle tree
Fagus sylvatica Beech
Fagus purpurea Copper beech
Ilex aquifolium (evergreen) Holly
Juniperus spp. (evergreen) Juniper
Ligustrum (evergreen) Privet
Lonicera nitida (evergreen) Chinese
    honeysuckle
Pittosporum tenuifolium (evergreen)
    Parchment bark
Prunus cerasifera Myrobalan
Prunus lusitanica (evergreen)
    Portugal laurel
Prunus spinosa Blackthorn
Pyracantha spp. (evergreen)

Buxus sempervirens
Box

Rosa rugosa Ramanas rose
Rosmarinus officinalis (evergreen)
Symphoricarpos spp. Snowberry
Taxus baccata (evergreen) Yew
Thuja plicata (evergreen) Western
    red cedar
Ulex europaeus Gorse
Viburnum tinus (evergreen)

INFORMAL
Arundinaria japonica Bamboo
Berberis darwinii
Berberis stenophylla
Bupleurum fruticosum
Camellia
Garrya elliptica
Griselinia littoralis
Hebe traversii
Lavandula spp. Lavender
Mahonia aquifolium Oregon grape
Olearia haastii Daisy bush
Osmanthus delavayi
Phillyraea decora Mock privet
Phlomis fruticosa Jerusalem sage
Photinia × *fraseri*
Ruscus aculeatus Butcher's broom
Santolina japonica Cotton lavender
Sarcococca Sweet box
Senecio
Skimmia japonica
Ulex europaeus Gorse

PLANTS FOR SPECIFIC SOILS AND LOCATIONS

The following lists encompass all types of plants from field trees down to flowering annuals. You will notice that many plants have a tolerance of different soil types and locations and that your garden's overall planting list is only made truly exclusive if your conditions can be considered extreme, such as a cliff top or a bog. I hope that this book shows that visually, a limited planting list can work for you, making your selection simpler and bolder.

MOIST AND SWAMPY

TREES

Abies spp. Fir
Acer negundo Maple
Alnus spp. Alder
Amelanchier canadensis June berry
Aralia spinosa Devil's walking stick
Betula nigra pendula Birch
Betula papyrifera Paper birch
Carpinus caroliniana American hornbeam
Cedrus deodara Deodar
Crataegus oxyacantha and forms Hawthorn
Eucryphia spp.
Fraxinus excelsior Common ash
Fraxinus ornus Flowering ash
Fraxinus oxycarpa Ash
Fraxinus 'Raywood' Raywood ash
Ilex decidua Holly
Liquidambar styraciflua Sweet gum
Liriodendron tulipifera and forms Tulip tree
Magnolia grandiflora
Mespilus germanica
Metasequoia spp. Dawn redwood
Nothofagus antarctica Antarctic beech
Oxydendrum arboreum Sorrel tree
Parrotia spp.
Picea sitchensis Sitka spruce
Populus spp. Poplar
Prunus padus and forms
Pterocarya spp. Wing nut
Pyrus 'Beech Hill' Pear
Pyrus 'Chanticleer' Pear
Salix exigua Willow
Salix lanata 'Stuartii' Woolly willow
Salix repens argentea Creeping willow
Sorbus aucuparia and forms
Taxodium spp. Cypress

SHRUBS

Andromeda polifolia
Arcterica nana
Aronia arbutifolia Red chokeberry
Calluna vulgaris Heather

Calycanthus floridus Carolina allspice
Calycanthus occidentalis
Cassiope spp.
Clethra spp.
Cornus alba Dogwood
Cornus alba 'Sibirica'
Cornus sanguinea
Coronilla emerus Scorpion senna
Coronilla valentina
Cyrilla racemiflora

Kalmia latifolia
Calico bush

Eupatorium cannabinum Hemp-agrimony
Kalmia latifolia Calico bush
Leucothoe spp.
Neillia longiracemosa Nine bark
Pernettya spp. Prickly heath
Philadelphus spp. Mock orange
Physocarpus opulifolius
Rhamnus frangula Buckthorn
Rhododendron maxima
Rhododendron nudiflorum
Rhododendron viscosum
Rosa filipes Rose
Sambucus spp. Elder
Spiraea spp.
Symphoricarpus spp.
Viburnum lantana Wayfaring tree
Viburnum opulus Guelder rose
Viburnum rhytidophyllum

PERENNIALS

Achillea ptarmica Sneezewort
Aconitum anglicum Monk's hood
Ajuga reptans Bugle
Anemone hybrids Windflower
Asarum lemonii
Astilbe spp. False goatsbeard
Barbarea vulgaris Common yellow rocket
Calla palustris Bog arum
Caltha palustris Marsh marigold
Cardamine pratensis Cuckooflower
Carex morrowii alba Blue grass
Cicuta virosa Cowbane
Cirsium dissectum Meadow thistle
Cirsium helenioides Melancholy thistle
Cirsium palustre Marsh thistle
Dipsacus pillosus Small teasel
Epilobium hirsutum Great willowherb
Equisetum telmateia Giant horsetail
Euphorbia palustris Spurge
Filipendula ulmaria Meadowsweet
Geum rivale Water avens
Glyceria maxima Reed sweet-grass
Gunnera spp. Prickly rhubarb
Helonias bullata
Heloniopsis orientalis
Hypericum hirsutum Hairy St John's wort
Hypericum tetrapterum Square-stalked St John's-wort
Iris foetidissima Gladwyn iris
Iris pseudacorus Yellow flag
Juncus articulatus Jointed rush
Ligularia spp.
Lobelia cardinalis Cardinal flower
Lotus pendunculatus Marsh bird's foot trefoil
Lupinus nootkatensis Lupin
Luzula campestris Field woodrush
Luzula sylvatica Great woodrush
Lythrum salicaria Purple loosestrife
Mentha aquatica Water mint
Menyanthes trifoliata Bog bean
Mimulus guttatus Monkey flower
Molinia caerulea Purple moor-grass
Myosotis scorpioides Water forget-me-not
Myosotis secunda Marsh forget-me-not

Peltiphyllum Umbrella plant
Petasites hybridus Butterbur
Phlox spp.
Polygonum bistorta Bistort
Polygonum milettii
Pontederia spp.
Primula bulleyana Primrose
Primula florindae Primrose
Primula japonica Primrose
Primula pulverulenta Primrose
Ranunculus flammula Lesser spearwort
Ranunculus lingua Great spearwort
Ranunculus sceleratus Celery-leaved crowfoot
Rodgersia spp.
Salvia uliginosa Sage
Sanguisorbia canadensis American burnet
Scrophularia auriculata Figwort
Scrophularia scorodonia Balm-leaved figwort
Scutellaria galericulata Skull cap
Senecio aquaticus Marsh ragwort
Senecio tanguticus Groundsel
Silaum silaus Pepper saxifrage
Spartina pectinata
Stachys palustris Marsh woundwort
Succisa pratensis Devil's-bit scabious
Symphytum officinale Comfrey
Trollius spp. Globe flower
Typha spp. Cat-tail
Valeriana officinalis Valerian
Verbena corymbosa Vervain
Veronica beccabunga Brooklime
Viola palustris Marsh violet
Vitis riparia Vine

COLD EXPOSED INLAND

TREES

Acer campestre Field maple
Acer pseudoplatanus Sycamore
Aesculus hippocastanum Horse chestnut
Alnus glutinosa Common alder
Betula pendula Birch
Carpinus betulus Hornbeam
Carpinus columnaris

Carpinus fastigiata
Carpinus purpurea
Corylus colurna Turkish hazel
Crataegus monogyna Hawthorn

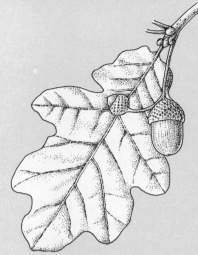

Quercus robur
Oak

Fagus sylvatica Beech
Fagus sylvatica 'Asplenifolia' Fern-leaved beech
Fagus sylvatica 'Dawyck' Fastigiate beech
Fraxinus excelsior Ash
Gleditsia triacanthos Honey locust
Larix decidua European larch
Ostrya carpinifolia Hop hornbeam
Picea sitchensis Sitka spruce
Pinus nigra Pine
Populus alba Poplar
Prunus lusitanica
Prunus spinosa
Pseudotsuga menziesii Douglas fir
Quercus robur Oak
Salix alba 'Caerulea' Cricket bat willow
Salix fragilis Crack willow
Sequoia sempervirens California redwood
Sorbus aria Whitebeam
Thuja plicata Western red cedar
Tilia cordata Lime
Ulmus glabra Wych elm

SHRUBS
Berberis spp. Barberry
Buddleia davidii Butterfly bush

Chaenomeles speciosa Flowering quince
Cornus spp. Dogwood
Corylus avellana Hazel
Cotoneaster (deciduous varieties)
Daphne mezereum Mezereon
Deutzia spp.
Elaeagnus spp.
Euonymus europaeus Spindle tree
Forsythia spp. Golden bells
Garrya elliptica Silk tassel bush
Gaultheria spp.
Hippophae rhamnoides
Hydrangea arborescens
Hypericum spp. St John's wort
Ilex spp. Holly
Juniperus spp. Juniper
Kerria japonica Jew's mallow
Lavatera spp. Tree mallow
Lupinus arboreus Tree lupin
Mahonia aquifolium Oregon grape
Mimulus aurantiacus Monkey flower
Nerium oleander Oleander
Pachysandra terminalis
Penstemon spp. Beard tongue
Pernettya mucronata Prickly heath
Philadelphus spp. Mock orange
Phillyrea angustifolia Jasmine box
Phlomis fruticosa Jerusalem sage
Phyllodoce spp.
Potentilla spp. Cinquefoil
Pyracantha spp. Firethorn
Rhododendron ponticum
Rhus typhina Sumach
Rosa californica
Rosa canina Common briar
Rosa rugosa
Rosmarinus officinalis Rosemary
Rubus spp. Blackberry
Ruta graveolens Rue
Salix spp. Willow
Salvia officinalis Sage
Sambucus spp. Elder
Senecio spp.
Solanum aviculare crispum
Spiraea spp.
Stephanandra tanakae
Symphoricarpus spp.
Ulex spp. Gorse
Vaccinium spp.
Viburnum davidii
Viburnum lantana Wayfaring tree
Viburnum opulus Guelder rose

SEASIDE

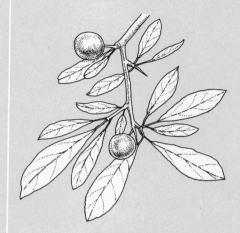

Prunus spinosa
Blackthorn

TREES
Acer campestre Field maple
Acer platanoides Norway maple
Acer pseudoplatanus Sycamore
Alnus glutinosa Alder
Betula pendula Birch
Castanea sativa Sweet chestnut
Crataegus monogyna Hawthorn
Fraxinus excelsior Ash
Ilex spp. Holly
Populus tremula Aspen
Prunus spinosa Blackthorn
Salix atrocinerea
Sorbus aria & forms Whitebeam
Sorbus intermedia Swedish whitebeam

SHRUBS
Arbutus unedo Strawberry tree
Arundinaria spp. Bamboo
Atriplex halimus Salt bush
Aucuba japonica
Berberis spp. (deciduous varieties) Barberry
Buddleia davidii & forms Butterfly bush
Choisya ternata Mexican orange-blossom
Cistus spp. Rock rose
Colutea arborescens Bladder senna
Cornus sanguinea Dogwood
Cotoneaster spp. (deciduous varieties)
Escallonia spp.

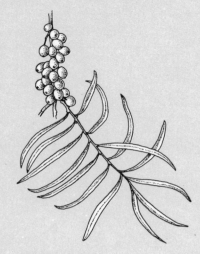

Hippophae rhamnoides
Sea buckthorn

Euonymus japonicus Spindle tree
Fuchsia spp.
Garrya elliptica
Genista spp. Broom
Griselinia littoralis
Hebe brachysiphon
Hebe salicifolia
Hebe speciosa and forms
Hippophae rhamnoides Sea buckthorn
Hypericum spp.
Olearia haastii Daisy bush
Olearia macrodonta New Zealand
   holly
Pittosporum spp. (green forms)
Pyracantha spp. Firethorn
Ribes sanguineum Flowering currant
Rosa pimpinellifolia Scotch rose
Rosa rubiginosa Sweetbriar rose
Rosa rugosa Ramanas rose
Rosmarinus officinalis Rosemary
Salix atrocinerea
Salix viminalis Osier
Sambucus spp. Elder
Senecio spp.
Spartium junceum Spanish broom
Tamarix spp. Tamarisk
Ulex europaeus Gorse
Viburnum lantana Wayfaring tree
Viburnum opulus Guelder rose
Viburnum tinus

PERENNIALS
Achillea millefolium Yarrow
Agapanthus campanulatus African lily

Allium cernuum
Allium christophii
Alstroemeria ligtu hybrid Peruvian lily
Anemone japonica Japanese anemone
Anthemis spp.
Anthericum algeriense
Armeria spp. Thrift
Artemisia spp.
Aster spp. (low growing) Michaelmas
   daisy
Bergenia spp.
Campanula spp. (low growing)
Catananche caerulea Cupid's dart
Centaurea spp.
Chrysanthemum spp. (low growing)
Crambe maritima Seakale
Crocosmia spp. Montbretia
Dianthus spp. Pink
Dierama spp. Wandflower
Echinops ritro Globe thistle
Erigeron spp. Fleabane
Erodium spp. Heron's bill
Eryngium spp.
Euphorbia spp. (low forms) Spurge
Filipendula hexapetala Dropwort
Geranium spp. Cranesbill
Gypsophila spp.
Heuchera spp. Alum root
Iris spp.
Kniphofia spp. Red-hot poker
Libertia formosa
Limonium spp. Sea lavender
Linaria spp. Toadflax
Lychnis flos-jovis Flower-of-Jove
Melissa spp. Balm
Mimulus spp. Monkey flower
Morina longifolia Whorl flower

Armeria maritima
Thrift

Nerine bowdenii
Oenothera spp.
Origanum spp.
Penstemon spp. Marjoram
Phormium tenax
Phygelius capensis
Physostegia virginiana False
   dragonhead
Polygonum bistorta Bistort
Potentilla spp. Cinquefoil
Pulsatilla spp.
Ruta spp. Rue
Salvia spp. (low growing) Sage
Santolina spp. Cotton lavender
Scabiosa spp. Scabious
Schizostylis coccinea Kaffir lily
Scrophularia aquatica Water figwort
Sedum spp. Stonecrop
Sisyrinchium spp. Satin flower
Stachys spp. Woundwort
Stokesia laevis Stokes' aster
Tritonia rosea
Veronica spp. Speedwell
Yucca spp.

GRAVEL

TREES
Acer platanoides Norway maple
Acer pseudoplatanus Sycamore
Aesculus spp. Horse chestnut
Ailanthus altissima Tree-of-heaven
Amelanchier ovalis
Betula pendula Birch
Caragana spp. Pea tree
Carpinus spp. Hornbeam
Crataegus monogyna Hawthorn
Fagus spp. Beech
Platanus spp. Plane tree
Populus spp. Poplar
Prunus avium Wild cherry
Quercus rubra Red oak
Salix spp. Willow
Sorbus spp. Whitebeam
Tilia spp. Lime

SHRUBS
Amelanchier lamarckii
Artemisia arborescens
Berberis spp. Barberry
Ceratostigma spp.

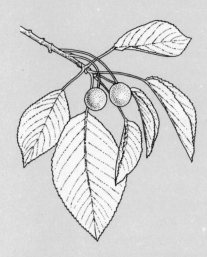

Platanus sp.
Plane tree

Cistus spp. Rock rose
Clerodendrum spp.
Cortaderia spp. Pampas grass
Corylus spp. Hazel
Cotoneaster spp.
Cytisus spp. Broom
Elaeagnus spp.
Elsholtzia spp.
Genista spp. Broom
Hedysarum spp.
Helianthemum spp. Sun rose
Helichrysum spp. Everlasting flower
Hibiscus spp. Rose mallow
Hippophae spp. Sea buckthorn
Hypericum spp. St John's wort
Iris spp.
Kniphofia spp. Torch lily
Lavandula spp. Lavender
Lespedeza spp. Bush clover
Perovskia spp.
Phlomis spp.
Potentilla spp. Cinquefoil
Rhus spp. Sumach
Rosmarinus spp. Rosemary
Salvia spp. Sage
Sambucus spp. Elder
Senecio spp.
Sisyrinchium spp. Satin flower
Spartium spp.
Spiraea spp.
Stephanandra spp.
Symphoricarpus spp.
Tamarix spp. Tamarisk
Ulex spp. Gorse

WOODLAND

TREES
Acer pseudoplatanus Sycamore
Alnus glutinosa Alder
Betula pendula Birch
Carpinus betulus Hornbeam
Corylus colurna Turkish hazel
Crataegus monogyna Hawthorn
Fagus sylvatica Beech
Fraxinus excelsior Ash
Ilex (green forms) Holly
Larix decidua Larch
Malus spp. Crab apple
Picea abies Spruce
Pinus sylvestris Scots pine
Populus spp. Poplar
Prunus spinosa Blackthorn
Quercus robur Common oak
Taxus baccata Yew
Tilia cordata Lime
Ulmus glabra Wych elm

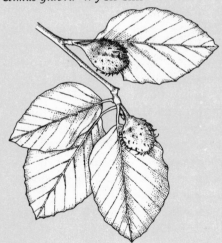

Fagus sylvatica
Beech

SHRUBS
Clematis vitalba Traveller's joy
Crataegus monogyna Hawthorn
Daphne laureola Spurge-laurel
Juniperus communis Juniper
Ligustrum vulgare Privet
Lonicera periclymenum Honeysuckle
Rosa arvensis Field rose
Rubus fruticosus Bramble
Ruscus aculeatus Butcher's broom
Salix cinerea Grey willow

Vaccinium myrtillus Bilberry
Viburnum opulus Guelder rose

PERENNIALS
Adoxa moschatellina Moschatel
Ajuga reptans Bugle
Anemone nemorosa Wood anemone
Buglossoides purpurocaeruleum
Campanula latifolia Great bellflower
Campanula trachelium Nettle-leaved
  bellflower
Digitalis purpurea Foxglove
Endymion non-scriptus Bluebell
Epilobium montanum Broad-leaved
  willowherb
Eupatorium cannabinum Hemp
  agrimony
Euphorbia amygdaloides Wood spurge
Fragaria vesca Wild strawberry
Galeobdolon luteum Yellow archangel
Galium odoratum Sweet woodruff
Geranium robertianum Herb Robert
Glechoma hederacea Ground ivy
Hypericum androsaemum Tutsan
Hypericum hirsutum Hairy St
  John's wort
Iris foetidissima Stinking iris
Lathyrus montanus Bitter vetch
Lathyrus sylvestris Wild pea
Linaria vulgaris Toadflax
Lychnis flos-cuculi Ragged Robin
Lysimachia nemorum Yellow
  pimpernel

Fragaria vesca
Wild strawberry

Melampyrum pratense Common cow-wheat
Mercurialis perennis Dog's mercury
Oxalis acetosella Wood sorrel
Primula elatior Oxlip
Primula vulgaris Primrose
Prunella vulgaris Selfheal
Sanicula europaea Sanicle
Stachys sylvatica Hedge woundwort
Stellaria holostea Greater stitchwort
Veronica chamaedrys Germander speedwell
Veronica montana Wood speedwell
Vicia sepium Bush vetch
Vinca minor Lesser periwinkle
Viola riviniana Common dog-violet

CHALKY SOIL

TREES

Abies grandis Giant fir
Abies koreana Korean fir
Acer campestre Field maple
Acer cappadocicum and forms Vine maple
Acer griseum Paperbark maple
Acer negundo and forms Box elder
Acer platanoides and forms Norway maple
Acer pseudoplatanus and forms Sycamore
Aesculus hippocastanum Horse chestnut
Ailanthus altissima Tree-of-Heaven
Alnus cordata Italian alder
Alnus glutinosa 'Aurea'
Alnus incana Grey alder
Amelanchier lamarckii
Betula spp. Birch
Caragana arborescens Pea tree
Carpinus betulus Hornbeam
Cedrus spp. Cedar
Corylus avellana Hazel
Cotoneaster spp.
Crataegus monogyna Hawthorn
Davidia involucrata Ghost tree
Fagus sylvatica Beech
Fraxinus excelsior and forms Ash
Fraxinus ornus and forms Flowering ash
Fraxinus oxycarpa Ash
Ginkgo biloba Maidenhair tree
Gleditsia triacanthus Honey locust

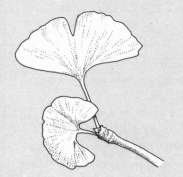

Gingko biloba
Maidenhair tree

Juglans spp. Walnut
Juniperus × *media* Juniper
Juniperus squamata and forms
Juniperus virginiana 'Grey Owl'
Koelreuteria paniculata Pride-of-India
Laburnum spp.
Liriodendron tulipifera Tulip tree
Magnolia kobus
Malus spp. Crab apple
Morus spp. Mulberry
Paulownia tomentosa
Populus alba White poplar
Populus canescens Grey poplar
Prunus spp. Cherry and plum
Pyrus spp. Pear
Quercus cerris Turkey oak
Quercus robur Common oak
Robinia pseudoacacia False acacia
Sophora japonica Pagoda tree
Sorbus aria and forms Whitebeam
Sorbus hybrida
Sorbus intermedia Swedish whitebeam
Tilia spp. Lime

SHRUBS

Aesculus parviflora Dwarf buckeye
Arbutus andrachne
Arbutus × *andrachnoides*
Arbutus unedo Strawberry tree
Arundinaria spp. Bamboo
Aucuba spp.
Berberis spp. (deciduous & evergreen) Barberry
Buddleia spp. Butterfly bush
Ceanothus spp.
Choisya ternata Mexican orange-blossom
Cistus spp. Rock rose

Clerodendrum trichotomum
Colutea arborescens Bladder senna
Cornus spp. Dogwood
Cotoneaster spp.
Cytisus nigricans Broom
Daphne mezereum Mezereon
Deutzia spp.
Elaeagnus spp.
Escallonia spp.
Eucryphia spp.
Euonymus spp. Spindle tree
Forsythia spp.
Fuchsia spp.
Hydrangea villosa
Hypericum spp.
Ilex spp. Holly
Indigofera spp. Indigo
Kerria japonica Jew's mallow
Kolkwitzia amabilis Beauty bush
Magnolia kobus
Mahonia aquifolium and forms
Olearia spp. Daisy bush
Osmanthus spp.
Paeonia spp. Peony
Philadelphus spp. Mock orange
Phlomis spp.
Pittosporum spp.
Potentilla spp. Cinquefoil
Prunus laurocerasus & forms
Pyracantha spp. Firethorn
Rhus spp. Sumach
Ribes spp. Currant
Romneya coulteri Californian tree-poppy
Rosmarinus spp. Rosemary
Rubus spp. Blackberry
Sambucus spp. Elder
Santolina spp. Cotton lavender
Sarcococca spp. Sweet box
Senecio spp.
Spartium junceum Spanish broom
Spiraea spp.
Staphylea spp. Bladder nut
Symphoricarpus spp.
Syringa spp. Lilac
Tamarix spp. Tamarisk
Teucrium spp. Germander
Ulex spp. Gorse
Viburnum spp.
Vinca spp. Periwinkle
Weigela spp.

EXTREME ACIDITY AND ALKALINITY

TREES
Alnus spp. Alder
Betula pendula and forms Silver birch
Crataegus oxycantha and forms Hawthorn
Fagus sylvatica Beech
Pinus nigra austriaca Austrian pine
Pinus sylvestris Scots pine
Populus alba and forms White poplar
Populus tremula Poplar
Quercus cerris Turkey oak
Quercus robur Common oak
Sorbus aria Whitebeam
Sorbus hybrida
Sorbus intermedia Swedish whitebeam
Taxus baccata Yew

SHRUBS
Cotoneaster spp.
Ligustrum ovalifolium and forms Oval-leaved privet
Rhamnus frangula Buckthorn
Salix caprea Goat willow
Sambucus spp. Elder

CLAY SOIL

TREES
Abies spp. Fir
Acer campestre Maple
Aesculus hippocastanum Horse chestnut

Picea breweriana
Brewer's weeping spruce

Alnus spp. Alder
Betula pendula Birch
Carpinus betulus Hornbeam
Corylus avellana Hazel
Crataegus monogyna Hawthorn
Encalyptus spp.
Fraxinus spp. Ash
Laburnum anagyroides
Malus spp. Apple
Picea breweriana Spruce
Platanus orientalis Plane tree
Populus spp. Poplar
Prunus spp.
Pyrus spp. Pear
Quercus spp. Oak
Salix spp. Willow
Sorbus spp.
Taxus baccata Yew
Thuja plicata 'Atrovirens' Western red cedar
Tilia spp. Lime

SHRUBS
Abelia spp.
Aralia spp.
Aucuba spp.
Berberis spp. Barberry
Chaenomeles spp. Flowering quince
Choisya ternata Mexican orange-blossom
Cornus spp. Dogwood
Cotoneaster spp.
Hypericum spp. St John's wort
Kerria japonica Jew's mallow
Osmanthus spp.
Philadelphus spp. Mock orange
Potentilla spp. Cinquefoil
Prunus laurocerasus and forms
Pyracantha spp. Firethorn
Rhamnus frangula Buckthorn
Rhododendron spp. (Hardy hybrids)
Ribes spp.
Rubus spp. Blackberry
Salix spp. Willow
Skimmia japonica
Spiraea spp.
Symphoricarpus spp.
Syringa spp. Lilac
Viburnum spp.
Vinca spp. Periwinkle
Weigela spp.

Chaenomeles sp.
Flowering quince

PERENNIALS
Acanthus longifolius
Acanthus mollis Bear's breeches
Alchemilla spp. Lady's mantle
Anemone × *hybrida* Windflower
Aruncus sylvester Goat's beard
Bergenia spp.
Brunnera macrophylla
Caltha palustris Kingcup
Carex spp. Sedge
Epimedium perralderianum Barrenwort
Eremurus robustus Foxtail lily
Euphorbia robbiae Spurge
Geranium spp. Cranesbill
Gunnera manicata
Helleborus spp. Hellebore
Hemerocallis spp. Day lily
Hosta spp. Plantain lily
Iris spp.
Lamium galeobdolon Yellow archangel
Lamium maculatum
Lonicera spp. Honeysuckle
Miscanthus sinensis and forms
Peltiphyllum peltatum Umbrella plant
Petasites japonicus
Phormium tenax New Zealand flax
Polygonatum × *hybridum* Solomon's seal
Primula spp. Primrose
Prunella × *hebbiana* Selfheal
Rheum palmatum Rhubarb
Rosa spp. Rose
Saxifraga × *urbium* Saxifrage
Symphytum grandiflorum Comfrey

Hemerocallis sp.
Day lily

Trachystemon orientalis
Waldsteinia ternata
Yucca spp.

LIGHT SANDY SOIL

TREES
Acer campestre Field maple
Acer ginnala Amur maple
Acer negundo and forms Box elder
Acer platanoides Norway maple
Acer pseudoplatanus Sycamore
Acer saccharinum Silver maple
Ailanthus altissima Tree-of-Heaven
Alnus cordata Italian alder
Betula pendula Birch
Caragana arborescens Pea tree

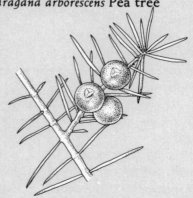

Juniperus sp.
Juniper

Castanea spp. Chestnut
Cedrus spp. Cedar
Cercidiphyllum japonicum
Fraxinus ornus Flowering ash
Gleditsia triacanthos Honey locust
Juniperus spp. Juniper
Koelreuteria paniculata Pride-of-India
Larix decidua European larch
Larix kaempferi Japanese larch
Pinus sylvestris Scots pine
Pinus maritima Corsican pine
Populus alba and forms White poplar
Pseudotsuga menziesii Douglas fir
Robinia pseudoacacia False acacia
Salix alba 'Liempde' White willow
Salix daphnoides Violet willow

SHRUBS
Amelanchier lamarckii
Artemisia arborescens
Berberis spp. Barberry
Ceratostigma willmottianum
Cistus spp. Rock rose
Clerodendrum trichotomum
Corylus spp. Hazel
Cotoneaster spp. (Prostrate)
Cytisus spp. Broom
Elaeagnus spp.
Genista spp.
Helichrysum spp. Everlastings
Hibiscus syriacus Rose mallow
Hippophae rhamnoides Sea buckthorn
Hypericum spp.
Indigofera spp. Indigo
Lavandula spp. Lavender
Lespedeza spp. Bush clover
Perovskia atriplicifolia
Phlomis fruticosa Jerusalem sage
Potentilla spp. Cinquefoil
Rhus spp. Sumach
Romneya coulteri Californian tree
   poppy
Rosmarinus officinalis Rosemary
Salvia spp. Sage
Sambucus spp. Elder
Senecio spp.
Spartium junceum Spanish broom
Spiraea spp.
Stephanandra spp.
Symphoricarpus spp.
Tamarix spp. Tamarisk
Ulex spp. Gorse

BADLY DRAINED SOIL

TREES
Acer pseudoplatanus Sycamore
Alnus incana 'Laciniata' Cut-leaved
   alder
Carpinus betulus Hornbeam
Davidia involucrata Handkerchief
   tree
Populus spp. Poplar
Pterocarya × *rehderiana* Wing nut
Pyrus spp. Pear
Quercus robur Common oak
Salix spp. Willow
Taxodium distichum

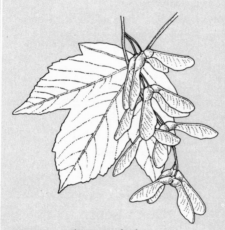

Acer pseudoplatanus
Sycamore

SHRUBS
Arundinaria vagans
Cornus spp. Dogwood
Rubus cockburnianus ulmifolius
Sambucus spp. Elder
Viburnum opulus Guelder rose

PERENNIALS
Glyceria maxima and forms
Gunnera spp.
Iris pseudacorus and forms
Ligularia clivorum and forms
Ligularia przewalskii × *hessei*
   'Gregnog gold'
Miscanthus sacchariflorus
Miscanthus sinensis
Petasites japonicus giganteus

INDEX

Page numbers in *italic* refer to illustrations and captions

ACKNOWLEDGMENTS

Author's acknowledgments
Without the help of Dorling Kindersley's in-house staff I could not have put this book together—for we have mutually beaten out the mores of the country mood through stimulating discussion and argument. I would like to thank, in particular, Meryl Lloyd and David Lamb both of whom I have enjoyed working with immensely. Jacqui Hurst's photography was a joy with which to work as well. I had invaluable assistance from my friend Sarah Broley in Washington DC, from Jane Pooley and of course, at home base, the efficient and relentless support of my secretary Jenny Paterson.

Photographer's acknowledgments
Jacqui Hurst would like to thank everybody who allowed her to photograph their gardens for this book: Janet Allen, Major and The Hon Mrs Arbuthnot, Elsie and Henry Ball, Ellis and Henry Bull, Tom Bartlett, Anne Belam, Bob and Penny Black, Alix Blomer, Mr and Mrs Blomer, Humphrey Brooke, John and Sheila Bruce, Mr and Mrs A J Buchanan, Anthony and Elizabeth Bullivant, Beth Chatto, His Honour Judge Clay and Mrs Clay, Mr and Mrs G Clay, Mr and Mrs G Goode-Adams, Dr and Mrs J Cox, Sylvia and Colin Dales, Ann Dewar, Lord and Lady Dickinson, Dale and Alice Fishburn, Mr D Flower, Gainsborough House Trust, Mr and Mrs I Garnett-Orme, Sir Julian Gascoigne, Mr and The Hon Mrs Peter Healing, Patrick Heron, Major and Mrs A Hibbert, Penelope Hobhouse, Judith and Simon Hopkinson, Mr and Mrs W Howes-Bassett, Barrie Hurst, Hazel Hurst, Mr and Mrs J Knight, Mr and Mrs R Marshall, Mr and Mrs R Merton, Joy Moss, Mr and Mrs Norton, Mr and Mrs Palmer, Mr and Mrs A E Pedder, Mr and Mrs F Plumb, Mrs Pumphrey, Major D and Lady Anne Rasch, Mr and Mrs C A Richardson, Martyn Rix, Rodney and Pamela Russell, Mrs Sedgwick, The Hon Mrs Smith-Ryland, Mrs Sybil Spencer, Dr and Mrs Stanton, John Tann, Mrs V. Thomas, Mr and Mrs J Thompson, Myles Thoroton-Hildyard, Mrs D Verey, Mrs C L Ward, Michael and Denny Wickham, Mr and Mrs David Williams, Mr and Mrs Wright; also special thanks to David Robertson.

Dorling Kindersley would like to thank:
The Royal Botanic Gardens, Kew, Hyams and Cockerton Ltd., John Tann, Martyn Rix, Richard Bird, Simon Adams, Arthur Brown, Tessa Richardson-Jones, Kate Grant and Jenny Engelmann.

Illustrations by Vanessa Luff, Eric Thomas, Vana Haggerty, David Ashby, Peter Morter, Rodney Shackell, Imperial Artists